HOW TO BE A SUCCESSFUL AUTHOR AND NOT LOSE YOUR MIND

THERESA HALVORSEN
S. FAXON

No Bad Books Press, LLC

San Diego, CA

NBBP

table of contents

Scan to access our blogs and other
helpful resources.

introduction

You are ready to write. You have your leather notebook or laptop in front of you, and you've just found the perfect spot in your favorite chaise lounge chair. There's only one problem; your toddler is screaming, your labradoodle is ripping a pillow apart, and your partner can't figure out how to use the air fryer.

They need you. Now.

We have *all* been there. We, the authors of this book, are authors with full-time jobs, relationships, human and animal children, and houses that *constantly* need our attention. So, how have we balanced our writing careers with all the rest? How have we produced several books, both those that we've written and others we have published for our authors under our imprint?[1] How have we been successful in our day jobs, maintained those relationships and been there for the immediate, "Mom, I need you?" Is there a secret sauce or some magic formula? And how do we do this without losing our minds?

Well, we've received these questions quite the lot, which is how the idea for this book was born. While we believe one has to have a touch of crazy to be an author, this book addresses the questions we hear regularly about becoming successful authors, including how to measure success.

We are firm believers that each person's journey will be different, but we hope our following tips, anecdotes, and exercises will help you on your path to becoming a successful author. When doing the exercises, find what works best for you; there may be an exercise or a section that you're not comfortable with. That's fine. But the goal of this book is to become a successful author and not lose your mind.

What's Ahead

We organized this book into seven chapters. The titles of these chapters are the questions we are most frequently asked and in these, we use sub-topics and various exercises to answer them.

1. Where and how do you get started?
2. How do you actually get published?
3. How do you find inspiration/ideas?
4. How do you stay motivated?
5. How do you actually sell books?
6. But there's only 24 hours in a day—how do you do all of this?
7. But how do you become a successful author?

We will answer these questions in depth, and, as you read along, think about how you deal with the topics we discuss. Are your tactics similar to ours, or are they different? And upon completing each exercise, CELEBRATE and give yourself a small reward. Yes! We believe in rewards, but more to that treat later...

We also want to acknowledge that people reading this

book may be at various stages in their writing career. There may be times that this text will feel very basic or there may be times you feel like a boss because you've already done a good number of the items we suggest. If one section seems too easy, bear with us and just skip on ahead or take part in the exercise to stretch those writing muscles out in ways they may not be used to. We also added some "advanced tips" throughout the book as well. We intend this book to be here to support you at whatever stage you are at, even if it's just to remind you that you are a writer and that's something pretty darn special.

As you go along in this book, take a stab at answering these questions by engaging with the various exercises (but please, don't actually stab the book.) And please, be honest with yourself. These exercises are for you and you alone. So find a fresh notebook that excites you to open up (you know what I'm talking about) or check out our I'm a Writer! notebook.

In the book, *Writing Alone, Writing Together,* by Judy Reeves, there is a fantastic section about "Claiming Yourself as A Writer," where Reeves says, "Until you name yourself Writer, you will never be a writer who writes (and keeps writing)."

So do it. Do it right now. Say it; "I am a writer." Even if you're reading this in a public place (we won't judge!). Say it loud, say it clear, say it from your heart. "I am a writer." Write this at the top of your notebook's first page and hold it tight. Writing is a part of who you are as a human being, so let's embrace and celebrate it!

Throughout this book, we reference several products and classes; we are not sponsored or affiliated with any. We are merely sharing our honest, and to be honest, biased opinions on the resources we have used that may be helpful for you on your journeys.

Alright, crack those knuckles, sharpen those pencils, do whatever it takes to get you into the zone (we have a section on this ahead as well), and let's do this!

Your Witty-Writing-Tour-Guides

Before we sweep you away on this magical adventure, allow us to introduce ourselves.

Theresa: *Oh lord, do I really have to do this? Yes? Ok, fine. I'm a fiction and nonfiction writer. I like speculative fiction, but will write whatever I feel like. What I really like are characters and unpacking the crazy layers that make up their actions. I love words and how different choices and combinations evoke certain feelings and thoughts. A joy is helping authors make their stories the best they can be and seeing their eyes light up when they say, "Wait! I have an idea!" I'm task and business-oriented and truly enjoy my to-dos in the publishing world. And I love talking about craft and industry. Which is all another way to say that I'm an author, the chief editor and co-founder at No Bad Books Press, LLC and a co-host for the podcast, Semi-Sages of the Pages. I belong to a lot of organizations, including San Diego Writers and Editors Guild, San Diego Writers, Ink, the Independent Book Publishers Association and I'm a chairperson of the local chapter of the Horror Writers Association. Most of the time, I'm overly caffeinated, at times drink too much wine and if you're on a call with me, you'll hear/see a random pet.*

Sarah (S. Faxon): *I'm an award-winning author and creative warrior, a moniker I earned for all of my various projects. On top of being an author of dark fantasy, urban fantasy, horror, and thriller tales, I'm a cover designer, a book trailer maker, and a terrarium/aquarium enthusiast. Are my terrariums/aquariums directly related to my writing? No, but I see crafting tiny worlds in* *contained spaces as an art form similar to developing a story. If I don't have pen ink on my hands or if I haven't spent at least fifteen minutes a day writing, it feels like my soul is missing something. Helping other writers on their journey and spreading the word of their tales to the world is something I love. I'm also a co-host in the writing podcast, Semi-Sages of the Pages. I am a member of the Horror Writers Association, the Independent Book Publishers Association, and San Diego Writers, Ink. With Theresa, I'm a co-founder and the Creative Director of No Bad Books Press, LLC and I regularly hear/see Theresa's random pets in Zoom calls. (Her cat mooned me on camera just the other day.)*

Between us, we have had a wide range of experiences in the writing and publishing industry and we've experienced both traditional and independent avenues. We are Yin and Yang companions in our small press; Theresa handles editing and the business side of things while Sarah handles the creative side, making us a dynamic duo in our industry. We have found a balance, granted a delicate one, between our "9-5" jobs, relationships, our writing careers all without losing our minds (mostly). We hope that in some small way, this book helps you to establish a balance that also works for you.

one
where and how do you get started?

"To know how to get started, you have to know where you're going."
-S. Faxon

BUCKLE UP. This is a long chapter. But creating a firm foundation will help you build a sturdy home.

Whether you're writing fiction or nonfiction, where to start is a multi-layered question and it's going to be different for every individual. So let's phrase this a different way—what are your goals as an author? In terms of goals, we've seen three general groups of authors.

- Group 1: You have a story in your heart you want to get on the page. This story is for your friends, yourself and/or your family. This goal is valid, wonderful, and beautiful, and there are many tools out there to help you with this. A couple of examples of this type of project are memoirs and fictional stories you told your children you'd like your great-grand children to read as well.

- Group 2: You'd like your writings to make some money, perhaps to equal what you spend on it, but you see it as a hobby or side hustle. You're not looking to pay the bills with it, but you are investing a fair amount of time and money on this nonfiction or fiction project.
- Group 3: Writing is your life. You not only want to pay the bills with it, you dream of going on book tours, having merchandise related to your books, and droves of fans who dress up like your characters on Halloween (this was actually a goal of Sarah's and she honest-to-goodness cried when she saw someone dress up like Gertrude from *The Animal Court*).

So this brings us to our first exercise (yes, we're getting started that fast!). Open up your notebook or laptop and let's take a moment to determine which group you belong to. (Psst—it's ok if you belong to more than one group for different projects. For now, let's focus on the project you're most interested in at the moment.)

Exercise (10 minutes): What are your Goals?

Now it's time for some stream-of-consciousness writing. Turn off your inner editor and loosely answer the following questions:

1. When you see the future, where are your writing and books in the grand scheme of your life? Do you see yourself writing every day, most days? Do you see writing dominating your life? Is thinking about writing, whether planning,

plotting, or talking out scenes with the characters in your head what you primarily do?

2. Who do you envision reading your books? Just your family? Anyone but your family? Strangers on the subway? Screaming fans ready to faint when you look at them?

3. Visualize your book(s) in your hand. What does it look like? What does it contain?

4. Are there many books, perhaps a bookshelf full of your books behind you, or is it just one title?

5. How many people are reading your books? Are you giving a speech about them, maybe answering questions about why a character made a certain choice that the reader disagreed with?

6. Are you being interviewed on the news, on podcasts and/or in newspapers/magazines?

Exercise (10 minutes): The Dose of Reality

Ok, we talked about the picture perfect life you're envisioning. Now let's talk about what's possible with who you are right now.

1. How much "free time" do you have or how much time are you currently devoting to writing? And don't worry if you think you have little time to spare or to dedicate to writing; later on in this book, we're going to teach you some strategies to increase your productivity and find pockets of time.

2. How much money can you devote to this? And it's ok if this changes over time or if you have

nothing to devote toward writing at this moment. This is an exercise to encourage you to have a budget in mind.

3. When do you want your author-future to be realized? Today, this year, in ten years?

4. Are you willing to keep learning and growing in areas such as craft, technology, publishing and marketing?

5. Are you willing to learn or do things you may not enjoy such as spreadsheets, data analysis or social media? Be honest. Knowing and setting the boundaries of what we don't want to do/don't have the bandwidth to learn is very important and will spare you from unnecessary challenges down the road.

We're going to refer back to the answers to these exercises a great deal during this book, so the more time you take to reflect on this, the better.

Why do we Write?

Before we wrote things down, we used oral stories and lessons, many of which have been lost to time. But at some point, some human drew on a cave wall with a bit of paint from stone, leaves and berries. Who was this human picking up a bit of bark and slate, or perhaps a singed piece of wood and forming letters? What were they trying to share?

- Teach an important lesson about survival?
- Warn others of what not to do, or what to do?
- Tell a story, likely working in the other two other bullet points, so the warning and the lesson stuck

with us?

Today, we know whatever drove these humans is likely the same thing that drives us today. These early writers wanted to do something more than just tell the stories; they wanted to show the stories; they wanted to keep the stories, the lessons, so one could look back and learn from them again. It's no wonder that books and journals were among many people's prize possessions, and why authors were and still are revered by many.

What do you want to Write?

Now that you've figured yourself out a bit, let's talk about your writing. There are a wild variety of stories, fiction and nonfiction out there. As you were visualizing yourself holding your own book up, was it one of the following broad genres?

- General nonfiction
- Fiction
- Memoir
- Literary
- Self-help
- Speculative fiction (horror, sci-fi, fantasy and all the sub-genres)
- Essays
- Poetry
- Mystery
- Crafting, cooking, photography, or other creative instruction
- Children's books (all ages–yes, young adult–and all the subgenres)
- Historical fiction and nonfiction

- Inspirational
- Romance (and all the sub-genres)
- Education, research, or knowledge
- Contemporary fiction (and all the sub-genres)

If you're not seeing your subject up there, that's ok. There are *thousands* of subjects, genres, and categories for books, so if you don't see paranormal women's fiction, don't worry—that counts under speculative fiction (for the sake of this exercise—delete that email). And it's also ok if you've combined self-help with memoir or horror with romance (*Theresa: hang on, that's an idea*).

Exercise (5 minutes): Picking your Genre

When picking up this book, some already know exactly what they want to write (such as shape-shifting blue aliens wearing kilts romancing contemporary women—and yep, that is a thing). However, others just want to write. They love the interplay of words and just want to have a book with their name on the cover.

So, for this next exercise, take a few minutes to write out what you want your book, series, or whatever to be about. Note, we're not talking about a plot summary or an outline. A stream of consciousness for a few minutes is fine.

You can skip this exercise if you already know what you're writing (yay! Free time!)

Finding your Ideal Reader

Theresa and Sarah took a class together about marketing and the instructors, Tamara Merrill and Jerry Strayve Jr. had an entire section, with homework, dedicated to finding our ideal reader. The first step to this is knowing your genre. As Sarah likes to say, "Know thy genre, know thy audience." (*Yes, she really says that.*)

Remember that exercise you may have skipped (*Theresa is terrible about doing exercises and validates your choices!*) to visualize who was holding your book? Ok, now's the time to remember that person or people.

Why do we want to know this, this early? It helps set up the success of your book if you target your reader partially through the writing itself. If you know who your ideal reader is, you can write the book to them. Think about it like this—if your ideal reader is seven, you don't want to write a two hundred thousand word hardcover book with teeny-tiny print that's full of cursing. That's an exaggerated example, so here's a more subtle one. Readers of romance expect a happy ending; if the characters you've built to have a steamy, passionate, happily ever after, end up never seeing each other again, those readers may feel disappointed and might not pick up your next book, no matter how beautifully written it may be. Knowing who your reader is helps you to craft the story that makes sense for your intended audience. It doesn't lay down a set standard of rules, but it helps you to know which tropes (genre stereotypes) to include and which to avoid based on your readers' expectations.

This also helps you to put together your marketing plan, but more on that later.

Ok, ready for another exercise?

Exercise (10 minutes): Find your Ideal Reader

This is based on a homework assignment given by Tamara Merrill and Jerry Strayve Jr. in *The Writers Crutch* marketing class. It may feel odd to imagine who your ideal reader is, but this will help you hone your writing and marketing plan to your desired audience.

- Male/female/not gender specific?
- Age range?
- Education level?
- Hobbies?
- Religion?
- Are they a parent or grandparent?
- Career/job/occupation?
- Where do they hang out?
- Do they like to travel?
- Do they have pets?
- Political views?
- Where do they live? Not only what part of the country, but rural? Urban? Suburbia?
- Do they live in a house or apartment? Do they own their house—do they care about owning their house?
- How much free time do they have?
- Do they listen to audiobooks or only have the time for novellas or short stories?

Ugh, Is it Time to Actually Write Yet?

Assuming you haven't already started writing your book/story, then yes, it's time! But there are more things to consider. These exercises may feel time consuming or restraining when all you want to do is write, but taking these steps is how we've "next-leveled" our writing careers.

Just a reminder, if you already have a finished product, are a published author or feel you have the basics down, skip ahead at any point. We won't be offended.

How do you want to Write?

We know there are people rolling their eyes, but some of you are saying, "Duh! With a pen and paper!" while others are saying, "On my phone in my notes app," while others are saying, "I dictate! Is there another way?"

Choosing what medium to write in can and likely should evolve. Some of you already know what works for you, so skip ahead. For those of you who prefer writing on a computer, do you use Word, Google Docs, Scrivener, Reedsy, Vellum, OneNote or Apple Pages? (If you use Pages, please let us know. We'd love to meet you.) There are pros and cons to every writing program and many writers have powerful feelings about their choices.

Word is great because everyone is familiar with it, and your editor and beta readers can use "Track Changes" for editing notes. If you're writing with other authors, Google Docs provides easy sharing access for those involved, can be edited on the go, and shares track changes like Word. We wrote this book and *Lost Aboard* using Google Docs because it's so easy to write in the same document at the same time. Theresa has a soft spot for Google Docs because it automatically saves (she's notorious for forgetting to hit save) and can access it easily from her phone when she's driving, walking or out and about. Don't ask Sarah about Word... just... don't.

But there are programs specifically designed for writers such as Scrivener (Sarah's favorite), Reedsy, Vellum, or Atticus. New programs are constantly arising, so if you're not happy with what you're using, there's bound to be a program just waiting to meet you! We love using Scrivener because it has a notecard section. Author programs like these are great because they can do the final formatting for you, if you're an indie writer, saving you valuable time.

For those that prefer to dictate, there are apps on your phone that can help and dictation programs such as Nuance Dragon, Apple, Google Docs, Braina and Otter. Scrivener also has a dictation function. Many busy writers have found dictation a great way to write while "on the road," but there's a learning curve associated and many writers find they need to spend more time editing their ramblings. For example, Sarah feels tongue tied when she tries to dictate her works, and swears that when she writes, her pen really does all the work and she just holds it.

Bottom-line—find whatever works for you. If your program isn't intuitive or if dealing with formatting issues becomes your primary focus over banging out your drafts, then it may be time to look for something else. Your writing program should help you stay in the zone and bring your world to life or answer those burning questions in your mind. If the word processor is taking you from those experiences, it's time to yeet that program into space and find something new.

Exercise (Dependent on you for time): Choosing Something to Write with:

If you want an exercise at the end of this section, take some time to do some research in what way of drafting you prefer. Experiment with them, many will offer free trials— PLEASE don't forget to cancel those if you're not a fan of them. But find what helps your thoughts to flow seamlessly!

Theresa: *I use a variety of tools for writing. I like to do my drafts in Scrivener because I like the note card function and that I can move scenes and chapters around. I also have a "cut" folder I use for when I cut scenes or sections I might want to use later. Then I use Google Docs for my editor and beta readers. Finally, No Bad*

Books Press, LLC uses Vellum or Adobe InDesign, depending on the project, for the final publication.

Sarah: *For years I hand wrote all of my drafts, then typed my stories in Word. I'd keep my notes in OneNote, or in no particular order in manilla files. It wasn't until recently I discovered the power of Scrivener and fell in love with it for the first drafts. I still alternate between Scrivener and a good old-fashioned notebook, which I always carry with me, but I am in love with the organization Scrivener provides. It has templates for keeping track of various character profiles, including a little area where you can paste an image of your characters for easy reference. Scrivener also has a wonderful notes section and, like Theresa, I love you can drag-and-drop scenes so easily. It helped me to organize twenty years of notes for my Blue Dragon Society series, which I'd almost given up on because of how complex my notes had become.*

Pro Tip: We have found formatting can become a little wonky, so we suggest waiting to make any major formatting changes until you're in Word, where you can then export to a final formatting program like Reedsy (it's free), Vellum, or InDesign. And also hit SAVE a lot. Not all programs auto save, so hit "Control S" as much as possible!

Craft and your Genre

Remember those exercises we did when we asked what your genre and ideal reader were? Now's the time to combine those pieces together because this impacts your readability, tropes, pacing, and even how long the story is. When writing a book, whether fiction, non-fiction, memoir, poetry or self help, it's important to submerge yourself within the genre. When Theresa wrote *The Dad's Playbook to Labor and Birth*, she read as many books on birth and labor that she could find. When Sarah started back into *The Blue Dragon Society* series, she dove into fantasy stories, legends, and lore. Diving into the contemporary titles of your subject helps you know what elements to include and exclude as you bring your manuscript to life.

What's a Trope?

Tropes are genre-based stereotypes. One of the most fun exercises Sarah does in the English Literature classes she teaches is having her students identify and provide examples of tropes in various movies based on the featured genre.

For horror, the characters almost always get separated, someone falls down running away in the woods, the lights always go out, the phones never work, and the sweet, grandpa types almost always die.

For romance, there's actually a formula - it's the pair meet, they fall in love, something breaks them apart, there's a grand gesture and then, by the end, they're kissing and it's happily ever after.**

For fantasy and all its subgenres, there's often a chosen one—that's why you see so many with a first person or a tight third person point of view. There's usually a sage, older character providing guidance, a healer of some sort, and a good vs. evil plot.

From mad scientists to mustache-twirling bad guys, tropes abound, but it doesn't mean you have to avoid them like the plague. Some are really fun and the readers expect them, depending on the genre. This is why those exercises of knowing the expectations of your readers and your genre are so important; there may be tropes they cannot live without and others that they'd rather die than read again. Or perhaps you could turn a trope on its head.

Dramatic? Likely. But we are fiction authors, after all…

Pro Tip: There are a TON of podcasts out there that talk about craft and marketing, and, as of publication time, here's a list of ones we enjoy that have been around for a while:

- Inside Independent Publishing with IBPA (focuses on publishing, but helpful for authors too)
- The Creative Penn
- Sell More Books Show
- Writing Excuses
- Story Grid
- And, of course, The Semi-Sages of the Pages

Finding and following blogs like Jane Friedman's who regularly report on what's happening in the industry are also invaluable resources for you to gather.

Elements to Consider for Nonfiction Informational/Self-Help/ Craft Books

Nonfiction books, like this one, require a distinct style of writing different from fiction. We intentionally chose a chummy and humorous style, rather than the style you might read in an epic fantasy or most post-apocalyptic pieces (were you laughing constantly when you read *A Song of Ice and Fire*? Or *The Hunger Games*?). Additionally, nonfiction, inspirational, self-help and crafting books are formatted differently, with bullet points, exercises and boxes around sections. Does your book need or have pictures like with craft or recipe books? Are they in color or will black and white suffice? Do you want drawings or pictures? And then what does your ideal reader expect? For cookbooks, most readers will want rich color, whereas a book explaining about DNA sequencing for neanderthals will have long paragraphs and lots of footnotes whereas a how-to book on crocheting might want step-by-step drawings.

These decisions come into play when you write your book, which is why it's important to have these in mind when you start writing. Familiarize yourself with comparable (comp) titles to your own works published within the last few years so you know what's trending, if your intent is to make money on the book you are producing.

A very important element to consider when drafting your manuscript is word count. If you have an intense self-help book, that's over 200,000 words, but you know it's going to change the world, consider cutting that book apart and releasing it as a series. We've included a list of word count expectations based on broad genres below. Of course, there are exceptions, but this is a part of why it's so worth the time to figure out what your audience is expecting. If you give them something way too long or way too short, they may be hesitant to buy or read it.

<u>General Nonfiction:</u>

- Standard: 50,000-80,000
- Self-help/How-do: 40,000-50,000
- Memoir: 60,000-80,000
- Children's: 500 - 3,000
- YA: 45,000-80,000
- Middle Grade: 20,000-50,000
- Chapter: 4,000-10,000
- Early reader: 200-300
- Picture books: 400-700

Elements to Consider with Fiction

With fiction, finding those comp titles is equally important. Stephen King is quoted as saying, "If you want to be a writer, you must do two things above all others: read a lot and write a lot." And we couldn't agree more with either of those ideas. Reading books in your genre will help you learn about expectations and could inspire various elements for your own works. Knowing the boundaries of your genre, or where your book can be found in a bookstore (fantasy, mystery, thriller), is a huge part of marketing and writing. The genre exceptions for a reverse harem romance will differ from a cozy mystery thriller. Not only will the style of writing be different, but the size of the paragraphs, the time you spend on description and what the readers expect will be different. A spy thriller may have an attractive main character, lots of nail-biting action that includes running, guns, and helicopters, short sentences and potato-chip chapters (just one more chapter! I gotta find out what happens!). But a cozy mystery may have longer chapters, more description, a main character that happens over a dead body, has a cat, and a romantic subplot with fade-to-black scenes.

And then genre can go even deeper. If you're writing fantasy, what kind of fantasy? Urban fantasy (like The Mercy Thompson series by Patricia Briggs or The Dark Elements series by Jennifer L. Armentrout) requires the story to start with bang, whereas an epic fantasy novel may start with a slow build (like *A Song of Ice and Fire* by George R. R. Martin—better known by its streaming show—*Game of Thrones*). Then there's dark fantasy, which Sarah writes, which includes more death, destruction and some horror elements.

Age and gender matters as well. Young Adult (YA) protagonists are younger (such as *A Pho Love Story* by Loan Le or *Divergent* by Veronica Roth) and have different character arcs than adult protagonists. Hard sci-fi protagonists may be alien, or living on a spaceship, whereas paranormal women's fiction protagonists are generally female and often kick-butt.

Epic fantasy stories may have a large cast of characters (*A Song of Ice and Fire*), and be full of unique species, castles and medieval outfits) whereas sci-fi may have a smaller cast and be set in space (*Project Hail Mary* by Andy Weir, for example).

Like with nonfiction, your genre also dictates your word count. Going outside of these "norms" makes it harder to find an agent/publisher and readers. Readers dictate what sells (ok, yes, there's debate, but this is not the book to talk about how the publishers control what sells—send us an email and we'll talk). The following are *general* guidelines. Yes, there are exceptions (delete *that* email!). If your book is considerably longer, consider breaking it into multiple books, which would give you a series (which is a great marketing tactic).

General Adult Fiction Word Count:

- Literary and commercial: 80,00-100,000
- Romance: 60,000-80,000 (some sub-genre romance fiction can go higher)
- Category romance[1]: 40,000 to 75,000
- Mystery and thriller: 70,000 to 110,000 (cozies like the Miss Marple series are more in the 60,000-80,000 range)
- Scifi-fantasy: 90,000-125,000
- Historical fiction: 80,000-120,000

Novellas and Short Stories (short fiction):

Novellas and short stories are shorter fiction of any genre. Novellas are around 35,000, but under 50,000 words, while short stories top out at about 15,000. There's also short fiction called flash, which is often a few hundred words. Short fiction can be of any genre and is a great way to explore your genre and find readers.

Editing/Beta/Alpha and ARC Readers

As an editor, Theresa is going to be firm on this: you need an editor. As an author, Sarah is going to be firm on this: you NEED an editor. You need someone who understands your genre to give you honest and direct feedback about your story. Yes, that can bruise, and yes, they might be wrong or may not understand your vision. Writing is a subjective craft open to interpretation. Additionally, if your goal is to sell a ton of books, a superb editor will look at the marketability of the book and may make changes with that in mind. So if your plan is to make this into a side gig or a profession, *please* get an editor. We all have typos. There are probably typos in this book, despite our editing process. We all make mistakes as authors—we all have a coffee in a cup on the desk in one paragraph that turns into tea in the next. It's *totally* ok to make mistakes in our writing and *no* first draft is perfect. We become blind to our mistakes as we edit our own work, which is why having a professional editor can take a book from being alright to award-winning.

There are generally three types of editors: developmental, line-by-line and proof or copy editors, though there is often overlap between the latter two.

- *Developmental* editors look at your entire story, the continuity of it and the character arcs. They will look at pacing from a wide-angle view and may offer suggestions such as increasing the romance between characters, tightening POV (Point of View) "cameras" or that an entire scene is illogical or doesn't advance the plot.
- *Line-by-line* editors look at your word choices, your pacing within the paragraphs, your sentence structure and eliminate wordiness and passive voice. They will look for continuity on the small ≠level such as characters' eye color and if the furniture moves during a scene.
- *Copy editors* are the grammarians, as Lynne Truss would call them, who help to ensure our writing is grammatically correct.

There are also proofreaders who look at the final draft of our manuscripts before they go to print to ensure that every element of your book is correct. We've heard legends of proofreaders who read a manuscript backwards and then from start to finish to ensure they catch everything. Now, if you're thinking, holy guacamole, that's a huge amount of editors, you're right. It is. But, take it from Sarah, who didn't use a genre specific editor with her first book and learned what happens when one doesn't have a proofreader or a line-by-line editor. Having this many editors seems like a LOT, but having multiple eyes on your manuscript develops a professionally made product beaming with the love you poured into it. Long story short, it takes a village.

Exercise (20 minutes): Feedback

We gave you extra time on this one so you dig deep. How well do you take constructive feedback? Be honest with yourself. If you have a day job and your boss mentions that you've had a lot of timecard corrections lately, and can you please remember to clock in and out, what's your reaction? Are you mortified? In tears? Angry? Obsessing over the interaction, what you said and what your boss said? Do you ignore the feedback? Do you make an effort to remember? Do you set an alarm on your phone reminding you to clock in and out or set up a sticky note?

Take the time to be truthful; these responses will tell you how you're going to react to your editor's suggestions. If you suspect you're going to respond with anxiety, depression or anger, inform your editor so they can work with you to ensure they're being truthful and constructive, but not hurtful. We'll talk about how to give and receive critiques in a few paragraphs.

To further develop your manuscript, you will also want

alpha, beta, and ARC readers. These are other writers or readers, familiar with your genre, who will offer you honest feedback about your book. When you actually get these suggestions within the timeline of your edits may vary and depending on the needs/goals of your project. We have included a general framework of when we ask for these types of readers. This is a gray area with some authors using beta readers before developmental editors and vice versa.

- *Alpha readers* are for when you're still in early drafts and they're looking at your overall story, plot and character arcs. They perform a similar purpose to developmental editors, but aren't professionals. At this stage, you're still willing to tear things down and do full rewrites if necessary.
- *Beta readers* are there when you're nearing the end of your story or feel it's mostly done. However, sometimes beta-readers will catch errors or make recommendations that may cause you to do a rewrite. Be prepared to tear down if necessary. Theresa's short story collection, *Tiny Gateways*, was delayed because her beta readers gave her some developmental suggestions that led to a full rewrite of two of the stories.
- *Advanced Reader Copies (ARCs)* are there when your story is done, but you're double checking for any continuity errors or massive plot holes. They're also there to give you those sacred early reviews and are very important to your marketing efforts (more on that later).

A word about sharing your works. You've worked hard

on your manuscript. It's your child. It's totally ok to be nervous about sending it out to people prior to it being published. There may be that fleeting suspicions in the back of your mind that one of your ARCs will steal your works and plaster it all over the internet, leaking your plot or claiming it as their own. This happened to Stephanie Meyer, after all, so why couldn't it happen to you? This fear is totally rational, but there are safeguards you can take to help protect your work.

Talk with your advanced readers about how you'd like them to keep the details or reviews of your work private until a desired date. Don't send them open documents—ensure your work is encrypted by using programs that allow people to download your manuscript as an .epub, something they can't print or distribute. If you're really worried, find a creative lawyer to help settle your concerns further.

Pro Tip: If you're wondering what program we use to safely share Advanced Reader Copies (ARCs), we export .epub files from Vellum and, as of the time of this publication, we use Bookfunnel which has helped to keep our ARC process safe, clean, and organized. Piracy sites are out there, and sometimes authors find their books for free from them. Be careful who you share .pdfs of your books with.

Exercise (5 minutes): Finding Beta Readers

Do you know anyone who could be a beta reader? And while friends and family are great, they don't count unless they're in the industry or prolific readers in your genre. If you don't... it's time to make some writer friends. See our section on writing groups in chapter four for how to go about this.

Pro Tip: Craft and writing inspiration books we recommend:

- *Writing the Breakout Novel* workbook by Donald Maass.
- *Story Genius* by Lisa Cron
- *Writing Alone, Writing Together* by Judy Reeves.
- Stephen King's *On Writing*

Critique

> "Is it dangerous or is it scary?"
> *-Stephen Green*

The dreaded C word: critique.

Receiving a "red-penned" document and going through the suggestions can be one of the most humbling situations authors deal with. Additionally, as we build well-rounded characters, we often pull from our own lives, thoughts and emotions. Sometimes feedback can feel like a personal attack on our own internal thoughts/feelings, especially if your editors/readers don't like a character. We've trusted our babies to someone else and seeing what they recommend to "improve" it can be pretty terrifying.

On our writing podcast, The Semi-Sages of the Pages, we did an entire series on giving and receiving critique. In the episodes, we discussed the top things to do prior to receiving critique, what to do while receiving it, and how to give it. While we highly recommend listening to those episodes, here are the highlights:

- When receiving critique, LISTEN, don't respond. Take a deep breath and make sure you're in a good headspace to receive the critique. If you're not, now's not the time. Reschedule or put the document down until you're feeling better.
- It's extremely difficult to hear people as they potentially offer feedback that changes that one line you thought was perfect, but, listen. They took the time to read your piece and to provide feedback. While you may not agree and may not do what they suggest, hearing them and not arguing with them does a few things:
- You may grow from the critique you are receiving. Good editors or advanced readers have experience and know-how and deserve to be listened to, even if you don't follow their advice. Beta readers may have less experience, but listen to them; you chose them because

they're readers in your genre and they may be right.

- Receiving constructive criticism with open ears is hard, but if you can do so without lashing back, they may want to work with you again. Our writing world is small and if a reputation develops about an author being difficult to critique, well, them rumors spread fast in the writing wild west.
- When giving critique, be honest, but respectful.
- Even if you struggled to get through the piece, help the author find what they can do to improve. There are no mistakes, only growth opportunities.
- Whenever providing feedback, consider including a clause along these lines: "My suggestions are just that; you may take them or leave them." There's even a lot of debate with copy editors around grammar. Just google the use of the Oxford comma.
- Try asking questions. It's a great way to highlight any issues without giving "criticism."
- Why did you make this choice?
- What in the character's background would cause them to behave this way?
- This character speaks very formally. Intentional?
- Several paragraphs ago, you said your main character gets manicures every week, but this line contradicts that

Finding an editor who you are comfortable receiving feedback from is extremely important. Likewise, if you work with an editor giving you feedback that is too abrasive, rude, or abusive (yes, we've heard horror stories), it's time to find a new editor. Don't feel like walking away from them is going to hurt their feelings. You need to find someone who you can talk out issues within your story and within your writing process. If the editor is unwilling to cooperate or work with you in these regards, walk away. There are plenty of editors out there who would love to work with you.

Sarah: *I've had beta readers rip apart my books and use fairly offensive language to describe exactly what they thought of some of my characters. Their words stung deeply, but I've had other beta readers provide constructive feedback about the same character, so between those readers, they helped to open my eyes to the shortcomings of the story, which I was able to fix. Moral of this story; even if the critique is hard, take a breath and don't take it to heart. There may be a sliver of something to it, even if you don't completely agree. Talk it out with the reviewer. And always ask for feedback from multiple people.*

Theresa: *As an editor, I'm a fan of the "is this intentional?" If the author says yes, I can explain why I tagged it as a potential issue, or I may just let it go. If the author says no, we can talk about it without them feeling attacked. An easy example comes from my Vella, Lying, Baking, and Surfing. One of the main characters introduced himself to Sabrina as Johnny, though his name was Jonathan. So in the chapters from Sabrina's point of view, I had to call him Johnny. In the chapters from his point of view, his name was Jonathan. A good editor would catch this early on and ask if it was intentional. And the answer is, yes.*

two
how do you actually get published?

"Publishing a book is like stuffing a note into a bottle and hurling it into the sea. Some bottles drown, some come safe to land, where the notes are read and then possibly cherished, or else misinterpreted, or else understood all too well by those who hate the message. You never know who your readers might be."

-Margaret Atwood

THERE ARE many paths to becoming a published writer. None are right and none are wrong. This book is about becoming a successful writer, and there is not ONE path toward that or one "real" definition of success. We've heard that one path makes you a "real" writer, while another does not. That's complete and utter bullshit. If you're writing, you are a writer. It doesn't matter what avenue you take to get published if it meets your goals. You're a freaking author. Celebrate that and don't let anyone tell you otherwise.

We are living in an incredible time where multiple avenues are now available for us to publish. The most well known is traditional, where one sends out queries and signs a contract with a publisher to receive a portion of the royalties. Then there's independent, where one does everything. And finally, a new third option, hybrid, where an author pays for services provided by a hybrid publisher and receives a larger share of the royalties. And then there are amalgamations of all three.

We'll talk a bit more about those paths in a few paragraphs... but first, let's talk about querying.

Querying in Brief

We will not go into great detail about querying as there are many other books, blog posts and articles about it. So in brief, querying means you're asking if an agent, editor, publisher, magazine, podcast, or blog is interested in your work.

For fiction, including short fiction, you have usually written the piece and are following submission guidelines outlined by the publisher. Submission guidelines often comprise:

- A cover letter explaining who you are and why you're submitting this piece.
- A specific word count of the story (between 5,00 and 10,000 words, unless instructed otherwise). For short fiction, use the complete piece.
- A 1-3 page synopsis of the work.
- A bio (often included in the cover letter).
- The genre of the book or who the book is meant for.

For nonfiction, you have not written the entire book and

are putting together a book proposal as outlined by the publisher. A book proposal often comprises:

- A cover letter explaining who you are and why you're submitting this piece.
- A bio that includes why you're the best person to write this book, your branding and any social media platforms
- The first three chapters.
- A 1-3 page synopsis/and or a chapter by chapter outline.
- A detailed marketing plan that includes information on where it'll sell, and your social media reach.

With querying, it's vital you follow the instructions of the publisher and include exactly what they're looking for. Doing more or less, assuming they will make an exception for your book, is a quick way to get a rejection. There are many publishers out there who will deny manuscripts for the smallest of details—don't let Times New Roman be what takes you down!

Traditional

In the traditional marketplace, authors query a publisher/agent/editor for a book deal, expecting to be paid a cut of the sales, called royalties. The traditional path is where many of the books in your local bookstore come from. This is where the "book deals" and advances come from. With many traditional publishers, you'll need to find an agent (yes, there are exceptions) before you can get that book deal from these publishers. Many people define "success" as a book deal. If that's for you, then go for it! There are a multitude of classes, podcasts, articles and books about achieving that path, and there's not enough space in this book to rehash those points.

The traditional path may lead to financial security and a "career," however there are *no* guarantees and many authors find financial security and a career on the other paths. The traditional path isn't easier or harder than the other paths; it's just different.

The traditional path is the cheapest of the options as querying doesn't cost you anything and the publisher does much of the marketing after you sign the book deal. Within the traditional path, there are many faces of publication companies. There are the Big Four/Five, (Penguin/Random House, Hatchett, Harper Collins, Simon & Schuster, and Macmillan), who carry a multitude of imprints beneath them.[1] These imprints are generally smaller presses, but small presses can be independent from the Big Five and are referred to as Indie/Independent Presses. The terms small presses/indie presses are used interchangeably, but they are not necessarily always the same. Confused? Don't worry, we all are. We'll take a closer look at the differences in a moment, which are up to date as of publication.

Small Press/Micro Press/Independent Publisher

A small press is a smaller publisher that doesn't have thousands of titles behind their name. A 2020 article published on Reedsy's blog defines a small press as a publisher making less than $50 million annually, whereas the big Four/Five make several billion.[2] A micro press only has a few dozen titles behind their name and publishes a few titles every year.

Many authors find a small press/independent publisher a good way to get their book published, as the competition is less fierce than getting published with the Big Four or Five. Small/indie presses are great places to learn about the writing and publishing industry.

Agents

While agents aren't publishers, they assist during the publishing process and many publishers, including the big four/five, require submissions be agented. An agent should be someone in your corner, fighting to get you a book deal and then continue to negotiate your contract and future book. They usually take 15% of your royalties and many authors feel they would not be as successful without their agent. Other authors feel an agent isn't necessary, and they were successful or will find success without one. To get an agent, you would query them, so do your research on how they like to be queried and their success rate.[3] We will not get into the weeds on agents, as there are many publications, websites, blogs, videos, articles etc. that already do that. And if you're interested in just the basics, Author's Publish released an article entitled, "How to Find the Right Agent for Your Book," by Emily Harstone, which provides great resources for vetting agents as well.

Hybrid Press

A hybrid press is an author subsidized model, where authors query and then pay for the services provided, which include publication and distribution. Hybrid publishers charge for their services before the book is published and some give the majority or all of the royalties earned back to the author. We feel hybrids should follow quality standards that make the book indistinguishable from traditional publishers. From the IBPA (Independent Book Publishers Association) website, hybrid publishers:

> "...behave just like traditional publishers in all respects, except when it comes to business model. Hybrid publishers use an author-subsidized business model, as opposed to financing all costs themselves, and in exchange return a higher-than-industry-standard share of sales proceeds to the author. In other words, a hybrid publisher makes income from a combination of publishing services and book sales."[4]

Our independent press, No Bad Books Press is a hybrid publisher and as members of IBPA, we take tremendous pride in following their mission, vision, and code of ethics, which include:

- Vetting submissions
- Publishing to industry standards
- Providing publishing
- Respecting the craft of authors, by paying higher-than-standard royalties

If interested, please review the article from IBPA regarding the definition of a hybrid press.

Indie/Self-Publish:

The indie or self-publishing path is perfect for those who want total control over their stories. Indie authors are the DIYers of the writing and publishing industry. However, while there are some that can build a house from scratch, there are others who can only fix a leaky sink, and others that can't even hang a picture straight. (*Theresa: do I own a tool box?*) There's no shame in being any of the above.

Some indie authors do it all. They do the writing, the editing, format the interior text, design their own cover, create their own imprint and might do Facebook and Amazon campaigns all by themselves. These indie authors might post three times a day on TikTok, write 5,000 words of their next novel and do a podcast interview, all on the same day. They are go-getters and take the time to learn every element needed to produce a book successfully.

If you whimpered a little reading that last paragraph, but still want to go indie, then that's when you look for help. There are people out there who have already dedicated hours to learning how to typeset covers, provide line-by-line editing, and assist with marketing. These professionals can and will help you with these items, including us.

Vanity Press:

A vanity press publishes all work for a fee. But wait, doesn't that sound like a hybrid press? Kinda. But vanity presses tend to just publish anything and there are often quality concerns. They tend not to care whether the book sells, they just publish it. Now, we do not want to discourage you from pursuing this as an option, if it calls to you. Like with anything else you invest in, be sure to do research on any publisher you go to. Look at the books they have published to see if their standards meet yours.

Your best resource for traditional publishers and agents is Publishers Marketplace. It's a giant website that tells you who is looking for what and what book deals are happening. It's invaluable when you're querying.

. . .

Exercise (10 min): Finding your path

Let's refer back to your goals.

- Who are you writing for?
- What are your financial goals?
- What's your time commitment to this industry? Be honest!
- How much do you want to spend on your business? And yes, now is the time to start thinking of this as a business.
- How much capacity do you have to dedicate toward learning various elements of the publishing process?

Take a few minutes to reflect on what you want, and what you can do for your business. And congratulations– you're on your path to becoming a business owner. Your book is a product and you are the owner, which makes you and your work a business. Whether you're pitching it to a publisher or you want to self-publish so your family can read it, it's yours.

Legal Stuff:

We are not lawyers, but a word about contracts. Whatever path you take, read over any contracts you receive carefully and pick your team with alacrity. You will need help from many to succeed, no matter how you define that. Again, it takes a village, and that village would highly benefit from having a lawyer. Before you sign ANYTHING, have a lawyer review the contract with you, no matter if you're going traditional, hybrid or hiring a cover designer. If there's anything in that contract that makes you uncomfort-able or if you're not sure about it, talk to the publishing company and/or a creative lawyer. Protect your work. It is yours and it is precious. Pay particular attention to what happens to the rights of your work if the publishing company should shut down. We've met many authors whose books have been "orphaned" because the presses who published them had to close. Some of these authors had their rights revert to them, others did not, so their books are stuck in limbo, unable to be seen or sold.

three
how do you find inspiration/ideas?

"You can't wait for inspiration. You have to go after it with a club."

-Jack London

MANY PEOPLE WANT to write a book, but don't know where to get started. As authors, we've taught our brains to "misbehave," and now have too many ideas. But it took us a while to get here. So this chapter is going to focus on where to find ideas and inspiration for that book you want to write.

Inspiration

The Oxford English dictionary defines inspiration "as the process of being mentally stimulated to do or feel something, especially to do something creative." As creatives, the sparks of inspiration lie all around us. In a Master Class lesson, David Baldacci explains that authors see the world a little differently. Instead of just seeing a coffee cup on a table, we think:

- What if the coffee cup fell off the table because of a nearby explosion?
- What if ripples started forming in the coffee because of a gigantic monster approaching?
- What if someone or something poisoned the coffee?[1]

Aside from possibly suffering from paranoia, authors are born with or can teach themselves how to have active imaginations. But sometimes it's hard to find inspiration for our current projects when we face that dreaded blank page, to say nothing about your kids screaming in the background, and receiving a nasty email from your boss.

Sarah: *As a fantasy author, looking at the coffee cup may not inspire 'what ifs,' but I do find myself staring at everyday objects, getting lost in the space beyond them as Euterpe, the muse, touches my shoulder to guide what'll happen next.*

Theresa: *As I'm a character-driven writer, I'm often inspired by unique people or situations. I enjoy playing the "tell-me-about-them?" game when I go out to dinner with my husband.[2] Some of those imaginings turn into characters in my stories.*

Many authors find inspiration in art, traveling, sitting in coffee shops, zoos, music, and in passing someone in the street and wondering what if. Other authors find inspiration in an event that happened to them, or with a memoir, many events that happened to them. Some authors find inspiration in wanting to help others, or share information and thus often get ideas through research or talking to others.

You can find inspiration and ideas all around you if you keep your eyes open and your mind clear. If you're finding those ideas but the words aren't flowing, what are you doing with your free time? Ideas are not created in a vacuum and often come from the subconscious. In Stephen King's iconic book *On Writing*, he says:

> "There is a muse, but he's not going to come fluttering down into your writing room and scatter creative fairy-dust all over your typewriter or computer. He lives on the ground. He's a basement kind of guy. You have to descend to his level, and once you get down there you have to furnish an apartment for him to live in. You have to do all the grunt labor, in other words, while the muse sits and smokes cigars and admires his bowling trophies and pretends to ignore you. Do you think it's fair? I think it's fair. He may not be much to look at, that muse-guy, and he may not be much of a conversationalist, but he's got inspiration. It's right that you should do all the work and burn all the midnight oil, because the guy with the cigar and the little wings has got a bag of magic. There's stuff in there that can change your life. Believe me, I know."

For many authors, ideas just kind of ooze up to the surface and if you don't catch them, wrestle them to the ground and try to collect that ooze into a jar (why did this analogy get so horrory?), you'll lose them.

In *Big Magic*, Elizabeth Gilbert feels ideas become self-aware to some extent. They float around, choosing the person to bring them to life. And sometimes, we have to tell them, no thanks. She talks about ideas as something that can be passed from person to person, especially if the first person isn't paying attention to them. This may explain why friends end up writing similar stories or having similar ideas.

Ok, so you have a fiction idea, now what? How do you

flesh it out into something grander, like a plot or an outline? On our podcast, The Semi-Sages of the Pages, M.S. Ewing, starts by asking five whys. Begin with a character or a setting and then ask why.

- Why is that character standing alone? Perhaps it's because he's waiting for his mom to pick him up from school.
- Why? Because she has to work two jobs, so she's not always there on time.
- Why? She has to work two jobs to support them because his dad doesn't get paid to do his job.
- Why? Because he's a superhero fighting crime and he doesn't have time for his family.
- Why? Because he's trying to make the world a better place for his son and doesn't realize that by not being there, he's making matters worse.

Now you have a story. Or at the very least, the beginnings of one.

Let's do this for nonfiction now. When proofing the book *Lost Aboard*, we were asked, why would someone pick up this book? What question are you trying to answer? That's the premise of a nonfiction book: you're trying to answer a question or a series of questions for a topic that you are an expert on. Perhaps, the market is missing the answers you've found and you want to fill that hole. For example, let's take Theresa's nonfiction book, the *Dad's Playbook to Labor and Birth*, and the questions Theresa asked when writing her book proposal.

- Is there a book for men about helping their partner through birth? There are, but they're very thick, and geared toward medication-free births.

- Do men want a book about helping their partner through birth regardless of medication? She asked her classes and got a resounding, "Yes."
- What are you including in this book? The guy's perspective! Tips for early labor, basics of supporting a partner through labor, such as breathing, massage and cool compresses. Stories from men about what they went through.
- How long should this book be? Very short, with bullet points, and quick, helpful tips.
- What would help readers enjoy this book? Lots of humor, and actual stories from dads and from my years of being a doula.

Exercise (10 minutes): The Five Questions
Fiction:

1. Right now, write the first name that comes to mind.
2. Now, imagine that person is running. From there, ask why and answer it.
3. From that answer, ask why, answer that.
4. Keep going in this exercise until all five of your whys are answered.

Bonus: Don't just stop at five whys. Keep going until you've run out of ideas.

Has a new story idea just emerged? Good! Add it to your idea list or just start writing.

• • •

Nonfiction:

1. What problem are you trying to solve or what information are you trying to share? Why?
2. Are there other books like yours? What makes yours unique?
3. What would be included in this book? What questions are you asking that others haven't before?
4. Do you have the answers and what resources do you have to answer them?

Keep this exercise in your pocket whenever you're stuck in a writing-rut. It comes in handy!

Sarah: *I get asked about where I get my ideas, a lot. I've been blessed and cursed with an overactive imagination. Sometimes when I'm smack in the middle of one story, characters from a totally different book will raise their heads and be like, "Um, excuse me, my scene is more important than theirs," and I'll have to oblige. My stories are constantly on my mind, but one thing that I find helps my pen to flow or my fingers to dance across the keys, is music. Music with lyrics inspires scenes, books, characters. A couple of examples - the songs "Radioactive" and "Demons" by Imagine Dragons inspired my character Laudine who shows up in many of my books. Mumford & Sons inspired a good part of my upcoming books, The Gorm Innis series.*

Theresa: *Conversely, I rarely get asked this question, probably because I'm always saying, "hang on, I just got an idea." I have an overactive imagination and am always seeing the world around me in different ways. Sometimes those ways scare me (there's a bush I pass by I know a monster (or maybe an alien... there's an idea) is hiding in).*

Working with the Subconscious

So how do you dig those ideas out of your brain? You know they're sitting there, you can feel them in the back of your head. How do you get them to bubble or ooze up to the surface? How do you get that muse to talk to you, or those guys in the basement to get to work? Well, you train your brain and your subconscious to push those ideas up to the surface.

- Setting. Try to write in the same place at the same time each day. This tells your brain it's time to write and helps to bridge that gap between the boys in the basement and the logical "me" brain (or as Freud said—the Ego).
- Move your setting. If the ideas and words aren't flowing, try moving to a different location. This is a favorite trick of Theresa's, though three of her writing locations are outside, which can frustrate her if it rains.
- Music. Music is a great way to focus the brain. In fact, for many, simply putting in earbuds can tell your brain and those boys in the basement it's time to work. Many writers will create playlists to help get them into the mood.
- Food. Our brains are weird, but specific flavors can help you focus and get creative. Sarah has different drinks for different books and Theresa always thinks about *River City Widows* when she eats jelly beans.
- Smells. Specific candles can set the tone and many authors will light a specific scented candle or burn incense to help them slip into their world.

- Try stream of consciousness writing. With this one, put a pen in your hand or fingers or a keyboard and see what comes out. No judgment or self-editing. Just write until you're done. You might be surprised,
- Sprints. This was a trick taught by someone on the Semi-Sages of the Pages Discord channel and related to the stream of consciousness writing. With sprinting, you set a timer and just start writing, trying to write as much as possible. Often your internal editor will keep their thoughts to themselves, thanks to this. Usually putting a hundred words down as fast as you can may unlock those guys in the basement.

One word about the subconscious: It's often doing things when you're not. So you may get your best ideas in the shower, while hiking or while at a work meeting. So keep that notebook or writing app close by to capture them.

Exercise (10 minutes): Getting that Subconscious to Work for you

Think back to when you had a perfect writing time, and the words were flowing with little help from you. Or that time you had a "I got it!" moment. What was going on around you? What smells, foods, sounds, feelings? Is this something you can replicate? If so, do the same thing and see if it helps next time you're stuck.

Taking Breaks and Other Creative Outlets

Hang on, we weren't talking about putting the book down (unless you gotta go do something, then go do it). We were talking about taking a break from writing and doing something else creative. Let the ideas, your muse or those boys in the basement, get to work when you're not paying attention. Anything that helps you think differently is a good thing. So pick up that guitar, try a puzzle, do a craft, or sew that patch onto those jeans. Doing other things not only improves your mental health but increases your creativity too.

Exercise (5 minutes): Choosing another creative outlet

Make a star, highlight, underline or happy face any of these. See if it helps you be more creative or unlocks anything you're stuck on. If not, then you just did some self-care and congratulations!

- Journaling with or without writing prompts
- Coloring an adult coloring book (they have ones with curse words and horror ones where you can scribble all the blood you want!)
- Legos
- Puzzles (interlocking ones)
- Crosswords or other games that require thinking differently
- Exercise, especially exercise with mental exercises such as yoga
- Going for a walk or drive (without listening to a podcast or book)
- Sewing, scrapbooking, making cards, building an invitation, etc
- Gardening
- Meditating
- Playing an instrument
- Video games

Turning Inspiration into Motivation

"I get a lot of letters from people. They say, "I want to be a
writer. What should I do?" I tell them to stop writing to me
and get on with it."
-Ruth Rendell

Ok, cool, you have an idea, it's getting fleshed out, but your
favorite show is premiering on Netflix and you have to
binge watch it before anyone else...

Pump. Those. Brakes.

We've been there! You have a story or an idea to
pursue, but there's a million other things that you want or
that *have* to be done first. Or maybe you don't "wanna", or
"can't." We'll talk more about how to prioritize in the time
management section, but this is an excellent opportunity to
check back in with your writing goals before you go flying
off into another project or get lost in a streaming show.

Flip the pages back in your exercise journal and highlight your goals. Write them down on a sticky note and post
them wherever you will see them every day. Those goals are
your motivation, your reasons to show why you want to be
a successful author. They're the whole reason you picked up
this book. This is totally subjective to you. And you are the
only one that matters. It's not about what other people
think or say, it's YOUR book. Let whatever reason behind
why you're crafting, sacrificing, researching, plotting, writing, be your driving force.

Now, try to identify for yourself your "I can't" vs. "I
don't wanna" moments. In the "I can't" camp, maybe you've
had a horrible day where your clients took absolutely every
part of you, your child was in detention, and your dog ate
the pack of the marshmallows you've been craving all day.

All you want to do is stare through the TV and occasionally blink. That's ok, those days happen to all of us. And those days fall under the "I can't" moments. Take a mental and emotional break; you've more than deserved it!

Then there's the "I don't wanna" moments. The, *I know I should write, but I haven't watered my plants today* or *my friends want me to join them at the bar later tonight.* Can the plants wait twenty more minutes while you bang out five hundred words on your laptop? If it's six o'clock and your friends want to go out at ten (you raging party animals you), can't you still squeeze in fifteen minutes toward your writing?

While these are extreme examples of "I can't" vs. "I don't wanna", take time throughout your day to identify those moments and keep your goals for why you are writing in the back of your mind. Think of your primary goal as your Peter Pan happy thought. Your primary goal will help make your story take wing and fly. And it'll help to get you through those days when you don't wanna or when you just can't.

Sarah: *I want to provide a reading escape for my readers and all I want to do is to make a healthy living off of being a writer and to play with plants (no joke, I literally decried to my living room, "can't I just write books and build terrariums, is that so much to ask?"). I don't want to have a nine-to-five job unrelated to writing. Words, characters, plots, and tropes are my world, my passion, and achieving that dream is my motivation. So as a reminder, on my desk is a framed tiny note one of my dearest friends wrote that says, "Sarah, congrats on your 1st book signing! Cheers to many more."*

Theresa: *So I'm an all-or-nothing gal. I'm 100% into everything I do. Healthy? Eh, but it's who I am. I decided to take writing seriously when I realized I was going to die one day and if I didn't get* *going on that writing thing, it wouldn't happen. Luckily, I found I adore every aspect of writing, from the act of putting words on paper, to editing, to publishing, to marketing and all the minutiae of tasks. It's never a chore and the "I don't wannas" rarely hit. I'm incredibly, phenomenally lucky to have found my passion and be able to make a living at it. It's the hardest thing I've ever done, but I treasure every moment.*

Exercise (Varies): Decorating your Goal

Grab one of your goals and spruce it up. In doing so, you'll be staring, writing, painting or carving those words and they'll get into your soul. You can try:

1. Write the words in a special style or ink and then frame them
2. Paint them on a stretched canvas frame and hang over your computer
3. Carve them into wood
4. Scrapbook them
5. Do a vision board
6. Write them out using skittles and take a picture (Yes, Theresa Gishes.)

While we would prefer you take the time to do this task yourself, if you want to pay someone to create a giant work of art, you hang over your bed, go for it. No judgment here!

four
how do you stay motivated?

"Without inspiration the best powers of the mind remain dormant. There is a fuel in us which needs to be ignited with sparks."
-Johann Gottfried Von Herder

YOU HAVE YOUR STORY. You have your whys—you know what you want, but that stupid blank page is staring at you, and oh look–is that dust on those blinds? Staying motivated to keep going when things get hard is a challenging part of being an author. But luckily we have some ideas that might help you, including goal setting, rewards and tasks you can try to increase your focus. Motivation and time management go hand-in-hand, so be sure to check the chapter on time management as well.

Setting Goals

We're not talking about the ones you just decorated. We're talking about smaller goals. Daily or weekly ones. And a great way to stay motivated when that blank page is staring at you is to set word count goals. NaNoWriMo (National

Novel Writing Month, often shortened to NaNo) was designed to help with this. During November (National Novel Writing Month), the goal is to write a 50,000 word novel by setting daily goals. There are trackers, groups and other authors to help cheer you on and many people find NaNo super motivating. They often continue daily word count goals after November.

> **Theresa:** *I spoke about my opinion of NaNoWriMo on a Semi-Sages of the Pages podcast, but felt it bore repeating. I love NaNoWriMo, but I see some behavior I wanted to discuss. NaNoWriMo is a self-imposed goal. Meeting that goal is not worth losing your partner, job, friends or family members over and yes, I see comments about that. It's not meant to affect your mental or physical health. If you want to stay up for 24-hours straight to type out fifty-thousand words, go for it, but you don't HAVE to. You don't get a prize, a book deal or money for completing it.*

If word counts don't speak to you (and they don't to Theresa) try setting other goals such getting a scene written, a character sketch done, or an outline completed. The key is finding a goal that works for you!

But it doesn't just have to just be writing goals; you can set goals for just about anything you want, including setting up Amazon ads, posting three TikTok videos a day or querying six agents every week.

So here are some tips on goal setting.

- Make sure they're obtainable. It may sound easy to write 5,000 words a day, but most authors have goals of 2,000 words a day, for a reason.
- Make sure you understand what completing that goal will take. Putting up three TikTok videos a

day sounds easy, but many find it hard to come
up with new ideas, film, edit, and post every day.

- What's the time commitment to your goal? We're
  going to talk more about time management in
  chapter six, but a huge part of making sure your
  goal is attainable is making sure you have the
  time for it.
- What's the financial ramifications, if any?
  Meaning, if you plan to post 10 Amazon ads
  every day, can you afford it?

Additionally, think about how rigid you're going to be
with yourself on meeting these goals. If not meeting the *self-imposed goal* will cause anxiety or depression, make sure
your goal is attainable. It's also ok to change goals. For
example, if Sarah has a word count goal of 1,000 words a
day, but went to Comic-Con, she may need to shorten it to
500 words for those days.

Here's another caveat about goals. Yes, you want to
meet them, but you want to meet them with some form of
quality (unless you're doing a sprint or stream-of-
consciousness writing) or you're just wasting your time. So
if you're staring at that blank page and something like this
comes out:

"The uncorny sprung to her golden feet thing (look up
real word later) and galloped through the oange field
going toward some castle (need to name) built of stone
(need to come up with color) heading toward the princess
(or maybe a prince, decide later) so that he (she/it?) culd
beat (how?) the angry witch…"

If you're doing the above to meet some word count
goals, consider taking a break. The above passage needs so

much editing you may be wasting your time, unless this is your process and then have fun! The same is true of social media or marketing. Breathe and put out quality work that matches your branding.

Exercise (10 min): Goal setting

- What are three goals you'd like to complete today?
- This week? This month?
- Are they obtainable?
- What will you do if you can't reach those goals?

Rewards

We've talked about goals; now let's talk about what you get when you meet them! Many authors, including Jonathan Maberry, use rewards to keep themselves motivated. In the monthly gathering he hosts in San Diego, the Writers Coffeehouse, Maberry has shared that he rewards himself with ten minutes of social media for every fifty minutes of work. He also puts money in a vacation fund when he completes his daily word count.

If you're rolling your eyes and thinking, "this is like getting a sticker when you answer a question in kindergarten." Yes, yes, it is. We are conditioned early on to expect something for good behavior, and in this context, is it really so bad to acknowledge our hard work? The key with rewards is to make them important to YOU. A day at the lake may sound amazing to one person and terrifying to another. Don't let anyone tell you what your reward *should* be.

Also, you don't have to do rewards for just writing. You

can reward yourself for completing editing, for doing marketing, for adding ten new amazon ads. This gig is hard and rewards are a great way to keep us reaching for all of our goals.

Even if you didn't achieve your daily goals, don't kick yourself. It's a self-imposed goal. Try again later. Also, if you've tied a reward that's self care (taking a hike, a quick snooze, getting a pedicure or taking a hot bath) to a goal, consider not denying yourself if you need it. You need self-care to function or you may make yourself miserable or cause a bout of depression.

Theresa: *I find rewards are a great way to stay motivated when things are rough. I will often use "just keep going until 8:30, then you can have a glass of wine" as a reward (oh, who am I kidding— I'm gonna have the wine anyway). I've also tried the ten minutes of social media as a reward to mixed results and it's something I should probably try again.*

Sarah: *I often reward myself with an hour of video games if I've met all the goals I've set for the day, but I really find working on my writing world to be a reward even though it is a lot of work.*

Here's how we suggest leveraging rewards so they're truly valuable.

- Set a clear, *attainable* goal and reward:
- If I write for twenty minutes without picking up my phone, I can have five minutes of TikTok time
- If I write two thousand words today, I will put five dollars in a vacation jar
- If I write a ten-minute sprint, I will add a cookie to my take-out order

- If I complete my monthly writing goal, I will reward myself with a nice lunch out

Ideas for Rewards

- A food treat you wouldn't normally eat or that you love, but is high in calories, high sugar, etc.
- A meal out, or a meal brought to you
- A self-care item like a massage, pedicure or lunch with a friend
- Money in an account for a future purchase
- Ask a partner for massages, etc.
- A few minutes with a video game, craft or favorite book
- Social media scrolling

Exercise (10 minutes): Choosing those rewards

1. Choose an attainable goal for the next time you write.
2. Then choose a reward to help you reach that goal.
3. Bonus: choose goals for the week or month with a larger reward to keep you motivated.

Increasing Focus

It doesn't do any good to create schedules and find pockets of time (see chapter 6), if when you sit down to write or edit you can't focus or stay motivated. So the next section is all about increasing your focus.

- Put down that phone! Seriously, hide it from yourself. Even if you hate the song you're listening to, just wait for it to end. Don't pick it up, or you may end up on social media or answering emails!
- Phones now have focus times you can set up in settings. Sarah silences her notifications and/or will leave her phone well beyond arm's reach in order to keep the interruptions at bay.
- Consider deleting the social media apps from your phone (yes, we understand that this is counterintuitive if you're trying to market yourself on social media, but we're talking about focusing, not marketing).
- Set a timer for social media time; honor it and get back to whatever project you're working on.
- Turn the Wi-Fi off so you don't get distracted.
- Pick a specific time to respond to your emails/texts/social media.
- Tell people not to bug you; find someone to watch your children/pets.
- Set contests/goals (see above section on goals)
- Theresa will often set project goals, such as finishing character sketches or getting through a certain number of pages on editing.
- Sarah sets one thousand word goals
- Sprint. Quality isn't the point here; it's about getting the words out. This can help if you're feeling a bit blocked or distracted.
- Sarah sets a timer for fifteen minutes and does not allow herself to do anything else but write during that time frame if she's struggling to get a story out or pulls the "I don't wanna".

- Meditate. Meditation can teach our mind how to quiet itself and focus on only one thing. This can help if you spring easily between projects (I see you with that phone, put it down!) or thoughts.
- Keep the momentum going. One thing Sarah and Theresa have found is if they take pauses from their writing, the momentum is gone. Not only might we have lost our passion for a project, but it's hard to remember where you left off, or those little nuances you tucked into chapter 3. Then you have to go back, reread or rewrite because you forgot about something. This wastes time. So try to not take huge breaks in the middle of projects, unless they're an intentional break to let a project breathe.

Sarah: *I've found that having one headphone in with the sound-track of whatever specific book I'm working on keeps me in the zone. If I don't have some sort of background music on, I get lost in my own thoughts.*

Theresa: *My phone is my own worst enemy and if I pick it up, I'll get lost in social media. I hide it if I really need to focus.*

Creating Rituals

One thing many authors do is start their writing time with a ritual. A ritual doesn't have to be religious or spiritual. It's just a process to tell your brain it's time to write. This is related, though different to working with your subconscious, because you are trying to write, not just daydream or think about your work in progress. A ritual can be just about anything you want it to be, as long as you repeat it each time you want to write. Here are a few ideas:

- A food item that you ONLY eat when it's time to write. Time to get out those jelly beans.
- A prayer, quote, a saying or a chant important to you
- Meditation (staring at a video of paint pouring/play-dough squishing etc. can count)
- Stretching/yoga/exercise
- Playing with a pet
- Getting dressed/ready for the day. In *Big Magic*, Elizabeth Gilbert talks about inspiring her muse by getting dressed up and putting on make-up before settling down to write.
- A shower, a bath, doing the dishes[1]
- Lighting a candle
- Getting your space set up. This may involve getting a cup of tea, your favorite blanket and that pen you love.
- Writing in the same place each day
- Writing at the same time each day

A few cautions about rituals, though. First, ensure its something you can actually do every time you can write. If your ritual is to take a long walk past a certain house in your neighborhood, waving to the hottie in the upstairs window *(Theresa: I need to lay off the romance novel writing)*, then you're going to find it hard to write on vacation when you can't wave to your hottie. Second, don't tie your creative pursuit so tightly to the ritual that you truly can't begin unless you do it. In On Writing, Stephen King talks a bit about how his rituals were completely upset when he was hit by a car. He couldn't even get into his writing space and had to move to a completely new location, which took some getting used to. Also, consider not making your ritual something addictive like alcohol. The alcoholic writer is a cliche, but it's also true (see Stephen King). If you can't write without that shot of whiskey prior, consider trying to find something else to create the same feeling or a way to trick your brain into thinking you received it.

Writing Groups

Joining a writing group can be another fantastic way to help you stay motivated and add a layer of accountability. Now, this does not work for everyone. If you're someone who loves a deadline or who works better when people expect to read something by a specific time, then this might be a great opportunity for you. No matter what your genre or topic is, there's likely a writing group for you. If you're not sure where to start, spend some time researching groups on Facebook within your genre. Like with just about everything else we've discussed so far, keeping your circle of people who are helping you develop your writing within your genre will help to identify beaten-to-death tropes or if something is missing. The people in these groups are authors, so they will understand dreading the white blank page. They'll hear your frustrations and hopefully be able to support you through those writer's ups and downs, like when your main characters are fighting you, or when you lost an hour to researching the exact synonym for "anger."

Writing or genre-centric conventions are also an excellent way to meet fellow writers. Back in 2019, we met Molly (M.S. Ewing), and Morrighan Puhr, and together formed the Semi-Sages of the Pages. We'd seen each other at various panels, and finally met for dinner after the first night. We compared notes of where we were in our writing journeys (pretty darn similar) and had similar thoughts about the lectures and panels we'd attended. Then Molly asked if we wanted to start a podcast. The rest is history.

Theresa: *That first night of the conference, I was feeling very alone. I had bonded with a few other writers, but they'd left and I was planning to order dinner and take it back to my room. Molly spotted me and asked if I wanted to join the other three for dinner. She still talks about how my face lit up. Molly's act of kindness changed my life.*

Bottom line, take steps out of your comfort zone and make those connections. Say, "hi, my name is _____, I write _____, what do you write?" Or "How did you hear about this conference?" Ask open-ended questions to make the spark of a conversation. The people you speak to may not become your instant bestie-writing buddies, but you'll never know unless you try.

Theresa and Sarah have been a part of many writing groups, and they want to give a special shout out to The Writers Coffeehouse, a nationwide group of writers that meet once a month. There are no fees, an active group on Facebook, and in the Southern California area, famed author Jonathan Maberry is the host. One of the things Sarah and Theresa appreciate the most about this group is that the authors who attend come from a diverse range of where they stand within the writing and publishing community, allowing people at the beginning of their careers to learn from those more advanced and for newer authors to share tips and tricks. It's a great symbiotic group, one that Theresa and Sarah highly recommend you seek, or even create in your community.

One thing we take great pride in is building writing communities. Throughout the year, we host several events, mostly via Zoom, bringing authors of various levels of their writing journeys together to network with one another and to learn from each other. This is one of our favorite ways to give back to the community because we remember what it was like to have no idea where to start or where to go. If you're interested in learning more about our marketing group, send us an email at nobbpress@gmail.com.

Now, for every amazing writing group, there are definitely bad writing groups, and it will take some time to figure out what'll work for you. Some groups will meet in person at the local coffee shop, some'll meet on Zoom. Some will meet once a week, others once a month. Each group will have different dynamics and different expectations. If this feels totally overwhelming, look back to our section on finding a critique partner as a base for finding a writing group that works for you. If you find one that looks good, ask the administrators if you can sit in before you contribute. Pay attention to if the group feels welcoming to you and the current members. Are they asking questions to help develop the craft of their members? Or does critique feel snippy, like they're just critiquing to critique? Is it even a group for critiquing or just for writing sprints? A bit of both? As you're trying to find what works for you, start by asking what you are looking to get out of a writing group and then grow from there.

Having a group to help keep you motivated and keeping your story a-flowing can be an excellent resource if that works for you. If reporting to your romantic partner your word count once a week is all the accountability you need, that's fantastic too. As we've stated ad nauseam, find what works for you.

Dealing with Mental Exhaustion

You've done all the rituals, you show up every week to your writing group, but you're staring at that blank page, and nothing is happening. The thoughts won't come. The guys in the basement are on strike.

This is real. We've all dealt with this. This goes back to that concept of *"I can't"* vs. *"I don't wanna."* This is an *"I can't,"* moment.

Mental exhaustion differs from not being able to stay motivated because you're distracted by social media, or kids, or a text message. And yet, being distracted and unable to focus can be a symptom of mental exhaustion. So can emotional instability; wanting to cry over everything or snapping at your kids for asking what's for dinner.

Mental exhaustion means your brain, your thoughts, are tired, and it's hard to create. Have you ever felt like you couldn't make another decision? Or like the idea of driving your child to a practice and making small talk with the other parents is too much, even if it's something you normally enjoy? Or do you drift away during a work meeting, but think of nothing? That's mental exhaustion. The COVID-19 pandemic taught us, among other things, the exhaustion of change and new thoughts.

But you can still create, or try when you're mentally tired

- Be kind to yourself. Perhaps rest is more important than trying to create.
- Try a sprint. Depending on your personality, either make it aggressive to see if the adrenaline helps, or make it easy and just try to get some words on paper or on your screen.
- Meditate. If you're not into meditation, this one can seem odd, but meditation can happen everywhere. Taking a walk while listening to peaceful music or no music can be meditative. There are also lots of free and low-cost apps that can help guide you too.

- Move for a few minutes. Head to the gym, jump around, go on a walk or dance like you used to when you were in middle school. Just move and see if you can get some adrenaline going.
- Try something else creative. Put your pen in your hand, on a piece of paper, and see what happens. Draw, paint, or use a creative app.
- Solve a puzzle. Again, this doesn't have to be a wooden or cardboard puzzle, but trying to solve something can help loosen things up. Building Legos counts, as does a puzzle game app.
- Put a time limit on your creativity. Give yourself thirty minutes and even if you only get ten words on paper, pat yourself on the back. You did great, pushing through exhaustion.

If you find yourself constantly mentally exhausted, it may be time to look around at your life. Are there things you can eliminate that you find mentally draining? Can you go down to a part-time job, or take a job that's less stressful? Have you said yes to too many things? Is there something you need to say no to?

Exercise (5 minutes): Working through Mental Exhaustion

Next time you think, "I should write," identify if your next thought is "ugh, but I have to do…" whatever it is. Stop and think to yourself–is this response an "I don't wanna" or is it an "I can't?" "I don't wanna" means you're being a normal person and your brain is creating distractions from sitting down and working on your project. "I can't" could be something like, "I just spent twelve hours at work and I don't have a brain cell left." There will absolutely be times when you can't and that is ok. We repeat—it is OK to be kind to yourself and rest when you need to. Remember, don't dismiss the importance of your mental health.

Dealing with Anxiety and Depression

Nothing can quite cut into your motivation like dealing with anxiety and depression. Both Sarah and Theresa struggle with anxiety and depression and Theresa struggles with exhaustion (*caffeine is not a food group, Theresa!*). These issues are something MANY creatives deal with, so we thought we'd take a short section to address it.

Important Note: If your anxiety and depression is ruling your life, or you're struggling with suicidal ideations or even suicidal thoughts, please reach out for help from your doctor, a friend or even the suicide hotline, 988.

Anxiety and depression can make it impossible to complete your goals. They make it harder for you to get up in the morning, to get through the day and to see reality (whatever that is to you).

> **Theresa:** *Sometimes you can use these emotions in your works. Kendle, my main character in* Warehouse Dreams *suffers from anxiety attacks. I found writing from Kendle's perspective while in an anxiety attack brought rawness and reality to this character's internal monologue. Those writings had to be heavily edited, but it helped me process the anxiety and created a fascinating and flawed character.*

> **Sarah:** *From the weight of lockdowns, isolation, civil unrest, and the pandemic, I wrote* The Complex, *which I lovingly refer to as my therapy book. In the paranormal thriller, I brought forward many real-life situations I'd encountered that I had to write about*

to process. Writing this story helped me to handle the chaos of an era we had absolutely no control over.

Imposter syndrome is another demon that haunts many of us creatives. While as of the time of publishing this book, imposter syndrome is not recognized in the DSM, it's a feeling of fraud despite having accomplished many things in a field. The feeling sprouts up when you compare yourself to others saying, *I know nothing compared to those experts; I don't belong*. This is different from normal anxiety you feel as you learn a new industry. However, when you've been in an industry for years and years and these negative thoughts arise, the American Psychological Association recommends talking to your mentors, to people who support you to help you out of these bouts of doubt.[2] In our Western culture, we are pressured to compare our achievements to those of others within our field, so it's of little surprise this feeling sprouts up within the writing communities.

Sarah has experienced these feelings of doubt multiple times when she's at conferences or when she's giving presentations; there'll be times it'll surface during her bouts of depression, until it tells her she can't and she shouldn't because she's not good enough, even though she has multiple titles published and has received awards for her writing. It's during these bouts where she cannot bring herself around to writing, to reading, or really doing much of anything beyond binge watching *The Golden Girls*. (The laughter usually helps to bring her out of these spirals, but not always.)

When you can't complete your goals because you just CAN'T (note: we're not talking about clinical depression or anxiety that can truly disrupt your life. We're talking about those hard days or weeks when everything seems too insurmountable), here are some tips to help you through:

- Let it go. Give yourself permission to stop temporarily. If your permission isn't enough, we give you permission. Go do something that makes you feel better. Take a nap, get a snack, go binge watch a show. How long do you take a break? Up to you. Take a break for an hour, an afternoon, a day, a week, etc.
- Try a sprint. If you're aiming to write 1,500 words today, set a timer for five minutes and see if you can write. If you can't, then let it go. If you can, either pat yourself on the back for writing for five minutes and move away or if you're feeling better, keep going.
- Try a change of scenery. Take a walk and try dictating your story (your neighbors already think you're nuts, don't worry about them). Find a park bench or a picnic table and try getting some sunlight and writing done out there.
- Eat healthy foods, drink lots of water, get some exercise (walks and cleaning work!) and get some sunlight. If you're in an area without sunlight, consider purchasing one of those sunlight lights. (Sarah had one when she worked in a windowless office and she really liked it!)
- Go do a hobby you enjoy. Water your plants, pet your cat, watch a streaming show or a movie you've been dying to see, read a book, etc.
- Clean. It's silly, but even washing one dish can reset your brain. And heavier tasks like vacuuming, can release endorphins.
- Cry, yell, curse and scream! These actions aren't promoted enough. We give you permission.
- Choose something on your to-do list you can do. If the idea of washing the dishes seems too much,

wash one dish. Walk out, get the mail, place it on your desk, but don't open it. Respond to one of the social media requests for your friendship. Then if it's too much, stop and go on to something you love.

- Know when your down times are. Theresa finds Friday and Thursday evenings on her way home from work very challenging. By this point, she's exhausted and stressed from the week. But she's learned that a good night's sleep usually fixes it all and come the next morning, she's ready to go.

- Plan something you can look forward to. This is the vacation benefit. Studies have found even just planning to go on a vacation can have stress reducing benefits.[3] But it doesn't have to be a vacation. Even planning to get a coffee with a friend or go for a pleasant hike can help.

- Call a friend or family member.

- Consider professional help. If you're constantly struggling to complete your goals due to anxiety or depression, look into what's causing it. Perhaps there are coping skills you can try with a professional.

Exercise (15 minutes): Getting through the "Grays"

This exercise helps us through the "case of the grays," as Sarah refers to her bouts of depression. If you're feeling blue or like you're an imposter, go back to why you decided you want to be a writer, not just what your goals are. Unless your goal is only to make money, let's stay away from those social trappings of the mansion in Hawaii over-looking the ocean, and the minions to do your every bidding. If there is no other driving force than making money to your writing goals, then skip this exercise (yay! Writing time!)

This reflection is more metaphysical.

- Do you love envisioning a different world?
- Do you love slipping into the skin and thoughts of another being?
- Do you love words themselves and how different words mean the same thing and yet evoke totally different feelings?
- Do you have wisdom you want to spread, lessons you wished someone had taught you?
- Do you have a calling to spread a message, something intrinsic that needs you to put words on paper?
- Is writing a part of your soul, a part of your self-care, a part of your healing?

Spend a good five to fifteen minutes writing every reason you write, because you're going to need this list when things get hard. And it's going to get hard sometimes.

Physical Health

We've talked about mental health, but taking care of yourself physically is also imperative. If you're exhausted due to sleep deprivation, your focus will be poor, along with the quality of your writing. Eating junk food and not exercising will also affect your focus, besides your health. When building your to-dos (more on that in the time management chapter), make sure you've included exercise and time to prepare or purchase healthy foods.

While neither Theresa nor Sarah have gym membership, both very much enjoy being outside. There's something that taps into our primordial souls about being outside —whether it's the air we're breathing or the sunlight on our skin, it helps us to clear our minds and think. Theresa takes her dog for a walk, or sits outside to work, while Sarah goes on bike rides. Taking these moments away from our desks and technology are like coming up for air after an arduous swim.

five
how do you
actually sell
books?

"You're selling the experience, not the plot."
-*L.S. Johnson*

NO MATTER how realistic you are, every author secretly hopes that once they or their publisher hit "publish" the book will magically end up on the "New Releases" table in every bookstore and be on the bestseller list all over the world. Oprah will feature your book in her book club and you'll spend months on a life-enriching, world book tour. Unfortunately, the reality is very different, regardless of the path you take toward writing.

But that's the dream, and while dreams are *absolutely* achievable, tenacity is the key. Being an author is not an immediate gratification process, even for those authors that hit the bestseller list on their first try.

It takes time. Tons. And work. More than you would imagine. It takes strategies that may work for some and not for you or may work for one book and not another. You may sell a hundred books in one day and then go for months without selling another. Selling books takes trial, error, and a great deal of frustration. And that's true for indie or traditional authors.

There are a few authors who have gotten a book deal on their first try that allows them to quit their day job. And there are a few indie authors who have sold thousands of books within a week of their debut release. However, even these authors say that these "wins" took tremendous amounts of work to achieve. Instant success caused other difficulties, stress, and several learning lessons. There are bestselling authors who still have day jobs, side-hustles, live with their parents and/or work eighty-hour weeks. Getting on that bestseller list doesn't mean everything is easy from here on out. It's just different.

Hacks, an Emmy Winning HBO show has a great quote from Episode 2 of the first season about how hard the creative life is. Debra, the main character, is a multi-million-aire because of her long career as a comic. She has a new writer, and the writer complains that this life is hard. Debra responds with *"You have to scratch and claw and it never f–king ends. And it doesn't get better, it just gets harder. Don't complain to me that I'm making your life **hard**. You don't even know what that means."*

The point is, even if you "make-it" on your first try, it's still gonna be arduous, painful and challenging.

Fiction

Most authors, indie or traditional, don't find their fan base until they have written between 5-10 books. If you're a fiction writer, it helps tremendously if those books are in a series. Readers enjoy staying with well-crafted characters and worlds. How many of you have cheered when your favorite author puts out a new book in a series you loved? Think how many times you've finished a book or a streaming show episode and then moved on to the next one, because you enjoyed it so much or just want to know what's going to happen next? For Sarah, she's read almost every book Dan Brown and Patricia Briggs have written. For Theresa, it's Ilona Andrews and Seanan McGuire. Sarah stood in line for hours waiting to get her pre-ordered copy of *Harry Potter and the Deathly Hallows*. We've all tagged along on the adventures of one particular author because we enjoyed how they wrote, their style, their story-telling vibe, and the characters we love. This is why having multiple titles can help to build an author's platform or brand.

So if one of your goals is to sell a lot of books, and another goal is to make a living as a fiction writer, consider creating a series and planning out your next five books. If you have multiple series ideas, plan those out too. That will help save you time.

And for those of you nonfiction writers tempted to skip this section, producing another book will help to build your resume as well. Is there a topic in your nonfiction book you want to explore further or a tangent your editor cut you can write another book about? Are you an expert in a related topic you can write a book about? Or can you intentionally plan your nonfiction book so you can pull multiple books out of that topic? Is your first book about a field that is constantly changing? How about a second edition? The possibilities for producing multiple titles for a nonfiction author can be just as achievable as they are for fiction.

Another selling strategy is to write books "to market" or "marketability." This works better for indie authors because they can move faster than publishers. Writing to market means studying the current landscape for fiction and nonfiction books and either writing to fill a gap, or intentionally writing in a "hot" field. So if blue-skinned alien romance books are flying off the shelves, starting to write a book about blue-skinned alien romance may miss the trend, but if you have one in your pocket that's ready to be released, hot dang, hit that publication button! On the flip side, if you have a weird western thriller that's ready to go during this blue-skinned alien romance craze you may have a harder time marketing or querying that series. You may want to put it away for a little while. But if multiple zombie regency romances (*Theresa: there's an idea!*) have hit the New York Times bestseller list and stayed there for several weeks, zombie regency romances might be something you can sell many books about IF you can do it fast and well. Pay attention to the trends and be ready to jump in if your niche genres catch fire.

Publishing and querying books fast and well takes strategy and a team of cover designers, editors, formatters and a street team for it to work. But many authors have done very well writing to market and riding those waves when they come. The same is very true of covers. If you're a DIYer, and you want to design your own cover, take the time to study the trends on the top 100 covers within your genre or similar genres. Stay up to date with what's selling. Something that would have been gorgeous ten years ago likely won't be considered eye-catching today.

Conversely, many authors have totally ignored writing to market, focusing on putting good books out there, generating fans who want THEIR unique genre, style or voice. They have their loyal fan base in their pocket and they have produced stories that fly. But wait, didn't we just tell you to study the market trends and now we're telling you the opposite could also lead you to success? Yep. We did. To be confusing, there's no right answer, or single path to success, which is frustrating and on several times we have cried to the heavens, "why is this so hard?!" Usually with an F word. This is why at the beginning of this chapter we stressed the importance of being tenacious. If you work hard to market your book, to bring the attention of your future readers that they *must* read this book, then the path to success is yours, regardless of if you write to market or not.

Nonfiction

In nonfiction, at the time of publication, Russia had recently invaded Ukraine, so books about war, the history of Russia, the history of Ukraine and even human rights are selling like crazy right now. If one of your goals is to sell a great deal of books, if anything relating to your particular field of expertise is anywhere in the news, consider jumping on that trend. You will increase your search engine optimization (the way people find you by Googling you) dramatically because you are addressing a topic or an issue that is in the minds of the public.

If you already have a book in a market that becomes "hot," it's time to intensify your marketing strategy. Consider giving it a new cover and a re-edit, especially if it's been several years since the original publication. If you went indie, this is a fairly straightforward thing to do as you have access to replacing your cover or the copy describing your book to reflect current trends. If you're traditionally published, reach out to your publisher to see if they'll invest in breathing new life into your book. If you can convince them your book might start to sell again or will sell better if they make some trending changes, they might listen. This is why being a global citizen is so important in our industries, whether nonfiction or fiction, as it keeps our eyes open to what's happening in the world and can help to make our stories soar.

Choosing your "Brand"

Influencers have brands, actors have brands and so do authors. In fact, a brand, whether or not you want one, is an important part of any marketing strategy.

Your brand is who you wish to present to the world. What parts of your personality/private life do you want to share with others? Gail Carriger, a novelist who writes primarily steampunk, has a powerful brand. She's tea-loving, corset wearing, carries amazing purses, and loves her cats. She seems to have a quirky and fun personality (*Theresa: I wanna be her when I grow up*). But choosing a brand as a steampunk novelist was very intentional for Ms. Carriger and it has helped her to sell many books and create a devoted fan base.

Dennis K. Crosby writes urban fantasy, but his brand focuses around being accessible and helpful to other authors. He also enjoys whiskey and cigars and uses this heavily in his branding. It's no coincidence that the main character of his *Death's Legacy* series also enjoys whiskey. Incorporating elements of your brand within your writing or vice versa is an excellent way to build a marketing foundation, allowing you to have seeds to grow your press kit or media kit.

> **Sarah:** *My branding has grown over the years, but, at publication, I can boil my branding down to this: helping fellow authors (such as yourself), all things fantasy, and my love of animals, plants, and nature. It's fairly broad, but it's aligned with my writing and things I like in real life. I'm also a video game playing nerd who loves Star Wars and is planning a Shire-Themed wedding for my fiancé and me. My author self and day-to-day self are the same. There are (some) elements of my life that are mine*

alone, but I'm essentially an open book, which is a part of my branding as well.

Many of my characters are interested in herbology and the powers within nature, and I'd like to focus more on that in my branding, but branding is something that evolves. It should develop with each new project you do.

> **Theresa:** You've likely noticed a part of my branding throughout this book: Sarcastic, irreverent and self-deprecating (I own a tool box and know how to use it). I use this aspect to increase my approachability so authors are more comfortable letting me help them, though it's also who I actually am. I'm a geek girl and attend events like Comic-Con and Wondercon and can rif about creating unlikeable characters using Wanda/Scarlet Witch as an example (see this Semi-Sage of the Pages podcast). My struggles with mental health are something I'm honest about. My jokes about being over-caffeinated are accurate. Like Sarah, I'm an animal lover, and often put pets in my works. If you're on a zoom call with me, you'll see my cats and may hear my dogs in the background. This is because they're pains and must interject themselves in all I do, but doubles with branding.

Exercise (20 minutes) Choosing your Brand:

Take some time to answer the following questions to help you develop your brand. And fall down rabbit holes. Stretch these questions, ask more and more. Visit our blog post, *Do Need to Build My Author Brand?*, to see Sarah and Theresa's answers:

- What do you enjoy doing?
- What are your hobbies?
- What are some unique things about yourself?
- What's your favorite food/drink? Do you drink alcohol? Tea? Coffee?
- What's your family like?
- Do you follow a religion? What does it teach you?
- Do you have a day job? What has it taught you, or what do you?
- What's your expertise in? (You don't have to write in that subject.)
- What do you want to share with the world?
- Do you have any writing routines to get into the zone?
- What does your living space look like?
- Who are YOU?

If you're a gun-touting, vest-wearing, motorcycle-driving, beer drinker, you won't be able to brand yourself as a quiet librarian wearing practical business suits that rides a horse to work every day (*Theresa: Hold it, I have an idea for a book!*). When you create your brand, you want it to be an element of yourself.

So take the time to really think on this one. Write down the answers to those questions then take a step back to reflect. When you're ready to return, ask yourself these questions:

- What do you write? Are there any echoes in what you write and your answers to the previous questions?

- Do you have any go-to genres or recurring themes? Do these echo in your personal life and the decisions you've made?
- What do readers of your genre/themes like? Are you like them? Do you have similar hobbies or interests?
- What do your characters like? What do they not like? How similar to YOU are your characters?

The answers to these questions will help you establish your brand and provide limitless possibilities of marketing content.

Your last step is to write three to five brief paragraphs/blog posts or even articles about something related to your brand; for Sarah, she could write about the power of plants, world building, or, maybe an article about how to be a successful author and not lose your mind... wait. Theresa may write a few paragraphs about her love for folk music, the random art she picks up at Wondercon/Comic-con or some time management tips. These paragraphs will help you form your brand, and root you so when people read or hear your name, they'll be able to connect those materials/subjects with you.

As a bonus, these also give you places where you can market you. Are you into bicycling like Catherine Pomeroy, author of *Four and a Half Billion People* is? Because of that, did you work it into your writing? If so, you can submit articles, blog posts and do podcast interviews about this topic, helping to establish your brand and market your work.

Congratulations! You now have the foundations of a marketing foundation kit. Summarize the answers you've written out in these past two exercises onto a single page, ideally bulleted, and keep handy for quick reference. Use these bullet points as seeds to branch out with content for your marketing. On the marketing kit, include the items you avoid like the plague to keep yourself within a defined marketing frame.

Developing a Marketing plan:

"In order to be found, someone has to be looking for you."
-*Stephen Green*

Search Engine Optimization (S.E.O) is a marketing term that essentially means if someone types in your name on Google, are they directed to where you want them to go? Is your website or your book page using relevant keywords about your genre or book title, so are you one of the first lines that pop up in Google's search results page? If not, let's crack those knuckles as it's time to do some marketing research work to improve your S.E.O. so people can actually find you.

The key to selling a lot of books is having a successful marketing plan or strategy for every book you write. Marketing is waving a flag with your book or your brand on it so that the world knows about it. Marketing is not limited to asking people to buy your book on social media. It's about being recognized in your branding, in your genre, in your field as an expert on that thing you specialize in. Being interviewed on a podcast, getting a four-star review or writing an article about that specific thing you're an expert on that appears in your third book, are examples of marketing.

In using the marketing and branding kit as the foundation to develop your marketing strategies, you will be spared the "OH MY GOD WHAT CONTENT AM I GOING TO CREATE???" troubles. Well, at least less of them. We recommend building a marketing kit for each one of your books and a marketing calendar. The marketing kit for your book is specific to those characters, that world, that plot and any interesting facts. It may feature writing articles about a particular theme within your story or showing character art of what you envision your main character to look like. Be specific but don't (we'll talk more about this later) just generate "Buy My Book" content. Develop a strategy that will make your readers fall in love with you and your characters so they will have no choice but to buy your book.

Newsletters

Many authors swear their success is directly related to their newsletters and the fans reading them. If you don't know, an author newsletter is an email that goes to subscribers telling them what you're up to, announcing any sales and asking them, nicely, to buy books, merchandise and other products. Almost every online business has a newsletter, regardless of the industry, which is why you may get a newsletter related to make-up after buying some nail polish.

Platforms for Newsletters

There are many paid websites that will help you build your newsletter and maintain your subscriptions. One tip is to make sure whatever platform you have is compatible with your website; that way you can have a pop-up on your website asking for people to sign up. As these platforms ebb and wan frequently, see our blog post, *Are Newsletters Still Relevant?*, for some more of our insights. However, GoDaddy (if your website is through them), Mailchimp, Squarespace (if your website is through them) and ConstantContact are some of the more famous and user friendly. If you sign up for a newsletter platform but you're not sure how to use it, look for a tutorial on YouTube.

Ensure you have the time and the bandwidth to dedicate to creating a newsletter or you'll waste valuable time and money. Newsletters only work if they're consistent.

Getting Subscribers

So you've gotten your newsletter platform and maybe even know what you'd like your newsletter to look like, you've watched the tutorials and you're ready to go. But you have no subscribers, other than your partner and parents. So naturally, we provided some tips to help you get people to sign-up.

- Offer sign-ups at various author events. Rather than using a hand-written list you have to download later, consider a QR code people can use to sign up on the spot. Put this QR code on everything from bookmarks, to postcards, to your business cards.
- Partner with other writers. This doesn't mean you share your list with them but offer to put their link in your newsletter, if they'll do the same for you. This is called newsletter swaps.
- Run ads on social media sites such as Facebook or Instagram.

- Offer a "magnet." A reader magnet is something for free you give to people who sign up for your newsletter. They're generally comprised an irresistible freebie which you can use programs like BookFunnel to facilitate. Good freebies include:
- A short story related to your character
- Holiday stories or stories told from the point of view of a side character are super popular
- An unpublished chapter of your best seller
- A free book they can't get elsewhere
- Tips/tricks related to your nonfiction topic
- Offer a giveaway such as a reading tablet or gift card. However, these subscribers may not be actually interested in YOU, just your giveaway. You may find your open rate drops, so use this one with caution.

What to put in your newsletter?

Cool, now you have 100 subscribers! Now what? Whatever you put in your newsletter, make sure it's tied to your brand. Pull out that marketing foundation kit you spent so much time developing and use that as a starting point to introduce your author-self to your audience. So if you use butterflies in your brand, your newsletter should have some element of a butterfly, whether it's a picture, an article about butterflies, interesting facts or simply a small clip art.

In terms of the copy and content for your newsletter, it will vary dramatically depending on your author brand, but in general consider including:

- Something topical. Something that happened in the news, a comment on a holiday or even the weather. See if you can tie this to your brand if possible.

- A comment or a few sentences on something personal, a project you completed, a dinner you enjoyed or something interesting your family or pets did.
- A call to action, or a reason to purchase your books. Perhaps you have a sale or can share a snippet of your book to get them interested.
- For nonfiction authors, include tips, tricks or interesting knowledge related to your area of expertise or your book.
- Many fiction authors will include book links to other authors' books (see above for newsletter swaps).
- Many fiction authors will also include writing or craft tips and tricks since readers are often writers too.

How often do you publish your newsletter?

There is some debate, but most newsletter experts recommend sending out your newsletter monthly, at least. Many authors send out newsletters weekly, though the sweet spot seems to be twice a month.

Maintaining a newsletter can be a ridiculous amount of work and it's something that if you start, you have to keep doing. You must release your newsletters consistently or your open rate will drop. Pick a day or a date and stick with it. For Sarah, unless she is extremely ill or has had a family emergency, she posts her newsletter on Monday nights so they're fresh and ready when people open their emails on Tuesday mornings. Every time she misses that post, at least one of her subscribers will check in on her within the week to ensure she's ok. This is a part of her "job" as she says to herself, so she is accountable for producing it every week. She even posts on vacation—one newsletter she wrote on a train in Ireland and another she drafted before, but sent from Main Street in Disneyland. Pick a date and a regiment that works for you and stick with it.

Here are a few examples of newsletter openings from authors across fiction genres. These examples only include the openings of their newsletters to give you an idea of the variety of formats and customizations available.

Monthly Musings

Hello friends! Another month, another newsletter! May has sped by and the summer is almost here! For me life has been a little crazy. My daughter just got her drivers' license this month, and my son is graduating from high school at the beginning of June! It's been hectic and a bit insane, but I wouldn't have it any other way.

On the writing front, my two stories on Kindle Vella are going strong! I'm about to upload episode 15 of 31, which makes it half way finished! The response to it has been really good and I've really enjoyed writing this cyberpunk series.

My fantasy story, Elements of Change about to get episode 8. I don't know how long this one will be, but I really enjoy exploring this world and its characters. I've got a lot to learn about it and can't wait to keep sharing it!

I'm also in the works for a few anthologies. I don't want to say too much, but I've got everything from steampunk to horror to fantasy to kids stories coming out! I love getting to dabble in so many genres and I'm really grateful for all the support I've gotten from my readers! Thank you for following me on my writing journey!

As busy as May was personally, it looks like June may calm down. Wrting though? Oh no! Look for a paranormal romance to come out on Kindle Vella. Love the fae? What happens when you marry one? Keep an eye out on my social media to see when you can get a peek at my newest serialized novel!

I hope June finds you safe and healthy! Keep writing, keep reading, and keep smiling!

Chris Bannor

This is an example of author Chris Bannor's newsletter. Note her branding in the header image.

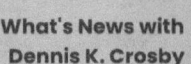

What's News with Dennis K. Crosby

The latest news with the author of Death's Legacy

Greetings, my friends! Man, it has been a busy 2021! Here's a quick recap...

In January, thanks to you, DEATH'S LEGACY began the year on the Amazon Bestsellers list. In February, I was one of three keynote speakers at the Southern California Writer's Conference. In that same month, I signed a contract to publish a short story in Volume 5 of the Castle of Horror Anthology. Then came March, where I signed a contract to publish my next book, Death's Debt.

We are rolling right along, my friends. There are some fun things coming, including: interviews, new releases, and a Death's Legacy Giveaway. I'm excited and hope you are, too. Strap in folks...

This is Dennis K. Crosby's newsletter opening. He includes an image of himself within his opening banner.

Burden of the Crown

This novel is a tale of two fathers. One who is acknowledged grieves for his lost son. One who is hidden grieves for what will never be.

I loved writing these heart-wrenching tales of men and their sons. With hearts as big as the sky, they act propelled by love for their child and the mother.

Here again, is a tale of two different loves. A king married to his land struggles with his duties as a husband. A concealed lover longs for any claims to his beloved.

I hope you savor the conclusion to my trilogy as much as I cherished writing it.

Read the conclusion to their story

Anna Bushi's newsletter includes images of her first three published books in the opening banner.

Welcome To The Newsletter!

Can you believe we're already over half way through the year? Where has it all gone? For me, it's been writing books and getting them ready for release, so I'm absolutely delighted that book two in my Empire Of Ruin series, Path Of War, is out today! Thanks for the response for arcs, and the interest you've all shown in it so far! It's currently #4 in the New Release charts on Amazon before its release day, which is pretty unbelievable! I'm incredibly proud of this book; it's bigger, larger in scope, and deeper than book one while keeping the fast pace and the intimate character moments people loved. I can't wait for you all to read it!

David Green has his custom branding at the top of his newsletter. You can tell with just one glance, that he's a fantasy author.

Exercise (10 minutes): Newsletters

The best way to learn about newsletters is to see one. Sarah has used Mailchimp for years to generate her newsletter. She addresses all of her letters with "Dear Readers," and uses a specific shade of pink for all the links within her newsletters. Take a moment to check hers and the others below for inspiration. Draft out how you'd like your formats to look to match your author brand. Keep your branding consistent, including the colors, graphics, and fonts so your readers will know at a glance that this email is from you and no one else.

Using Ads

There are A LOT of strategies for using ads to sell books, and many opinions about them. We're going to brush the surface in this section, but we highly recommend you take a class/webinar in doing ads. It can be very expensive, confusing and may not be successful if not done correctly.

There are several places authors have found success in placing ads.

- Social media platforms (TikTok, Facebook, Instagram)
- These are different than postings on these sites
- Amazon ads
- Newsletter sites such as BookBub, The Fussy Librarian and BookDoggy

The more books you have, "the more bang for your buck" with ads, especially if they're in a series or related somehow. If you've done a good job on your first book in a series, many readers will keep buying the rest of the series, even without an ad trigger.

Here's how that works. If you've spent $2.00 for an ad and have five books in your series, and a reader buys all five, you've made a significant profit, which Mark Dawson calls "Leveling Up". It's important to focus your ads on the first book in the series, though that doesn't mean you can't run ads on sequels. But readers don't tend to buy the 3rd book of an unfamiliar series and may click away, costing you money, without seeking your first book. (Theresa hears you ad experts shouting that this is wrong. We're scraping the surface with the basics of ads here and don't have the space to get deep into this. Delete that email!)

Your "copy" or the words used on the ad itself are vital.

Writing the best 3-5 sentences to entice someone to click on your ad is an art and takes a long time to learn. Set aside some money so you can learn this art, through trial or error, or plan to hire someone to help you write ad copy.

You will need to figure out keywords specific to the ad platform. Keywords are how the platform targets the people who might buy your book. There are programs such as PublisherRocket that can help you find the best keywords and apps that allow you to "scrub" the keywords of various sites. Full disclosure, we are not an affiliate of Publisher-Rocket, but we have found it to be very helpful.

Be aware of a time commitment. Ads work the best if you can run experiments on your copy, keywords and categories. It will take a long time to figure out the best ads, and you will have to pivot constantly.

If you're going to do ads, build a budget that works for you. It's easy to just keep adding more money to ads because they seem like small amounts, but can add up (pun enjoyed but not intended) quickly. Decide a point where you will stop the ads if they're costing you money, and you're not selling any books. HOWEVER, you will have to spend money before you see any sales. Just keep all of this in mind. Creating fastidious notes tracking your data on what works and what doesn't is invaluable.

Pro Tip: As you're generating ads, make one change at a time to help you narrow down what works in ads and what doesn't.

The more educated you are about the ads of your choice, the better they will go. Take the time to thoroughly learn a platform and run experiments before giving up.

> **Theresa:** I recently got into Amazon ads and I'm totally addicted to the experimental portion of the activity. If I use this copy and this combination of keywords, combined with this bid... what happens? Ok, If I use a different copy and the same keywords, with the same bid... what happens? As of publication, No Bad Books Press, LLC has some limited success with Amazon ads, but the learning curve has been expensive and time-consuming.

Websites

Every author needs a website they can send their readers to, especially if they're querying. Most websites are pretty affordable, though. Some authors have gotten away with using free blog websites, but we recommend finding a site that works within your budget and that looks professional.

If you're going to have a website, here are a few basics to include:

- A consistent "look" to the website. Sarah has a low clutter, clean style to her website and Theresa plays with textures to evoke emotions.
- Who you are, paying attention to branding.
- This is done through a brief bio page that includes:

- Your publications, even if they're not related to what you're trying to sell
- Something personal–kids, pets, where you live, what you like
- Other things tied to your brand, such as whether you enjoy cigars, bicycling or spend your time in competitive debate
- 1 or several headshots
- **Pro-tip!** Many authors doing many media outreach have several bios so the people interviewing them can choose their favorite based on their focus/word count See our blog post, *A Fifty Word Bio is All You Need, But…*, for some examples.
- Your publications
- Direct sales, the reader purchasing directly from you, allows you to keep the highest cut from your sales and is a strategy indie authors use. Sites like BookFunnel can help you set up ebook downloads directly from your website. If you're traditionally published, include links to your publisher or other platforms such as Amazon or Bookstore.org.
- Your media
- You want some sort of page that explains to readers where you'll be, and where you've been. If you have a lot of events coming up, please plan to put these on your website.
- A blog
- Your blog can mimic what's in your newsletter if you have one, but it's vital you blog. This keeps your website fresh in the Google algorithms and keeps your fans wanting to come back for more.
- Anything else you do

- If you have a podcast, an editing position or teach classes related to your topic, this is the place to put it, along with some interesting tidbits of information

Exercise (10 minutes): Building a Marketing Plan

You knew it was coming. Now's the time to start your marketing plan. This is just the beginning though and there's going to be more to fill in. Use your goals, your ideal reader, your author kit to help you in this section.

- Who are you? What's your author brand?
- How are you going to find readers?
- Newsletter?
- Events?
- Ads?
- Website?
- Social media? (More on that later.)
- What's your marketing budget?
- When will these things be completed and by whom?

Marketing and Where you Publish the Book

Ok, phew, now that we're out of those weeds, let's take a step back and talk about where you actually publish.

If you're a traditional author, then feel free to skip the next few paragraphs about WHERE to publish your book.

At publication time (and this changes constantly) there are two general strategies for publishing: go exclusive with Amazon, called Kindle Unlimited (KU) or publish in various distributors including IngramSpark, Barnes & Noble, Kobo, Draft2Digital, Smashwords, (at publication time, Draft2Digital and Smashwords have merged though a still have separate websites) Google Play and a multitude of others. This is called going "Wide".

KU is a subscription service readers pay Amazon for. Readers can download books for "free" after paying their subscription fees. KU readers are often voracious readers and may read several books a month, a week or even within a day. KU is a good way to establish your brand, especially if you're a romance author. Authors are paid in page views. There is a great deal of fine print with KU you should research. Of prime importance, **you cannot have your book published anywhere else if you're in KU** and Amazon will suspend your account if they find your book elsewhere. We cannot emphasize the importance of understanding this.

However, you can take your book off of KU and then go wide, but there's some fine print here too, so do your research.

There are pros and cons to each method that affect your ability to sell books.

Pros to Going "Wide"

- Your book is available everywhere online someone might purchase from, making it easier for readers to find it.
- Each distributor has marketing strategies, discounts, codes for free books etc. that can help with your marketing plan.
- If something happens to your books/account at one place, your book is in other places for readers to find.
- Some readers feel passionately negative about Amazon and won't buy books from them.

Cons to Going "Wide"

- It takes time to publish and maintain in all different distributor platforms, though they generally have similar requirements.
- Learning the different marketing strategies for each distributor is time-consuming and may prevent you from targeting one strategy.
- Many readers of genres such as romance, urban fantasy, paranormal romance, and historical romance expect the books to be available in KU and may not purchase your book from Amazon or anywhere else, if it's not in KU.

Pros to publishing in KU

- Depending on your genre, it may help new readers find you, especially if you're a new author.
- KU offers many marketing options and is supportive of their authors in KU.
- Using email marketing services such as BookDoggy or BookBub who target readers, do better when books are in KU, though there are exceptions.

Cons to publishing in KU

- If something happens to your Amazon account, your book is "gone" and not able to be purchased elsewhere. If you lose your Amazon account for breaking the rules, you cannot have any future indie published books in Amazon, though you can petition for reinstatement.

- Payment is… trickier. Some authors do very well getting money for page reads. Others don't and get more money from the book sales. Of note, you can still have people purchase your book through Amazon, both ebook and paperback, even if you're in KU.

Sarah: *At the time of publication, my books are wide EXCEPT for my urban fantasy, Blood Lords. I decided to use Vella, a new branch of Kindle Direct Publishing (KDP), because it's a serialization publication, which is perfect for the binge readers of urban fantasy. It's also a new platform, and I wanted to talk about it from personal experience if asked. So far, it's been a fun experiment. I've learned a lot from a craft standpoint about keeping sentences tight and building tension at the end of each episode so they are cliffhangers.*

That being said, I'm a big believer in having options as a reader, so I wanted to give that option to my readers.

Theresa: *At time of publication, my books are Wide, other than my stories in Vella. I prefer this option because I want all readers to have access to my books regardless of where it's published. Additionally, I'm not convinced the page read method of payment is the most lucrative. However, if I was to write a historical romance or a genre that readers prefer to be in KU, I might consider it.*

Distribution

If you're traditional, keep on skimming.

If you go through a traditional publisher or independent publishers, they have distributors who ensure books get into the right places. A distributor is a "middle man" who has built relationships with booksellers and may assist publishers in getting books into booksellers hands. Of note: while Smashwords and Kobo are considered distributors, these aren't the kind of distributors we're talking about.

IngramSpark is considered a distributor and used by indie authors and publishers. Booksellers purchase the books wholesale and IngramSpark distributes them. If your book doesn't sell, booksellers can return the books (if you've chosen that option), and then your payout from IngramSpark is affected. But on the flip side, many booksellers won't take a chance on your book if they can't return it.

Events

Traditionals, stop here! You may resume reading now...

Not to brag, events are one of areas No Bad Books Press, LLC have *thrived in*. Sarah and Theresa both love doing book events and because we publish speculative fiction, we love those geeky conventions! Events are great ways to not only sell books, but build newsletter subscribers, increase your brand and network with other authors. But it's not as easy as just showing up; there are a few things you need to do to maximize your time and energy at events to ensure you sell the most books possible.

There are many places out there, other than bookstores, you can sell your books at. Book fairs, conventions and book signings are the most obvious, but there's also farmer's markets, trade conventions, or crafting events that might be right for your book, especially if it's nonfiction. Farmer's markets are great for children's books, and pumpkin or Halloween-themed events might be great for horror books. Book festivals are great for all books, and horror, sci-fi and fantasy books sell well at those geeky conventions. So it's best if you choose the right convention for you and your books.

However, counter-programming can work well too. This means you may set up at a craft event, focused on crafts to sell your books. Wait, but isn't everyone there buying crafts? Yes, but there are no other booksellers to compete with. You may do well, you may not. Knowing your audience is the key in counter-programming. If you're at a craft event, who else is likely there? Women, right? So romance might do well. Bottom line, don't discount an event with a cheap table, just because you don't think readers will be there; readers are everywhere.

But naturally, it's not enough to just choose the event. There's more than just showing up with your boxes of books and cash box. For some large events like Comic-Con and Emerald City, you have to apply for the table and it helps if you have a large backing of conventions under your belt.

Additionally, events aren't free, so a budget is vital. The following are some things to consider if you're going to do an event.

- Table fee. Table fees can range from a few dollars to several thousand dollars. The more famous the event/convention, the more expensive it is. If your table fee is $150 and you're selling your books for $10 each, you will need to sell 15 books to make back just your table fee.
- Books. You will need books to sell. It's best to maximize your money and shipping costs by ordering as much as you can afford in a single shipment. However, you will then have to keep inventory and store your books. Keeping inventory is harder than you would think and

time-consuming (as Theresa's husband keeps
asking when she's going to find a different place
for the boxes of books).

- Table items. You need to make your table look
  appealing and there's a wide range of necessary
  items.
- Table cloths
- Banners marketing you for the table, behind the
  table, the side of the table etc.
- Book displays
- Display items. This should be branded to you
  and your books. We've seen lanterns, jewelry,
  ravens (not real!), beads, flowers, greenery,
  cardboard cutouts of characters, etc.
- Swag (more below)
- Marketing materials
- Business cards, postcards, bookmarks, etc.
- Bags for people to put your purchases in
- Swag or the free stuff you give away to get
  people to remind you once you're done. All of
  this stuff should be branded!
- Bookmarks—the cheapest and most popular
  giveaway
- Postcards
- Pens
- A craft item related to your branding/book or
  character. We've seen small ravens, beads or
  even coasters
- A giveaway item for newsletter sign-ups
- Payment collection
- For credit or debit cards, Square is the most
  popular, with Venmo (at publication time) being
  the second. There are fees associated with both,
  so make sure you include it in your budget.

- You will need a phone or iPad unless you spring for the company's devices. And Wi-Fi is helpful too.
- Cash and a safe place to put it. Consider bringing $100-$200 in low bills to give change. It also helps if you round book prices to end in a 5 or 0 to help with change. Theresa has attended many conventions where she's had to beg the concession stand and other participants for low bills, so think about how long the convention is when deciding how much cash to bring.
- Theresa and Sarah use a cash box for money, but you don't have to. Some authors use pockets, plastic bags, fanny packs or even a lunchbox. Just don't keep it on the table.
- Maintenance items. These are things you need to set up your table or your set-up will frustrate you and you'll have to make friends with other participants.
- Some way to put up your banners. This may vary depending on the location so be ready with magnets, clips and string.
- Tape, paperclips, scissors, pens, post-it notes, etc. The scissors and tape are the most important.
- Charger for phones.
- Extension cords and/or a power strip if you have electricity. Some vendors will hook up lights for evening events and use portable batteries for the electricity.
- Signing pen for signatures. Some people just use a basic pen, others will use a fancy one. Consider your branding on this!

Also, don't forget to budget for food, transportation and if it's a multiple day event, hotel fees. Staying with a friend or bunking up can help, as can bringing your own food.

Here are a couple of photos from tables at a few events that we have participated in:

Sarah at the No Bad Books Press indoor ComiCon Special Edition Booth.

Booth at outdoor North Bark Book Fair.

WonderCon booth with, Left to Right: M.S. Ewing, Dennis K. Crosby, and Theresa Halvorsen.

But How do I Sell Books at Events?

There's more to being successful at events than just showing up. You can't sit behind your table and wait for people to come to you. You have to interact, sell your books and sell yourself. Come up with a table pitch for each of your books, a few sentences max. Smile, and be prepared with that swag to draw them in. The worst thing you can do is sit behind your table and wait for people to come to you.

It's also nice if you have a buddy to help you too. Conventions can be lonely and it's hard to take bathroom/food breaks if you're by yourself. If your table gets busy, it's harder to assist everyone by yourself and a buddy may help prevent theft.

Pro Tip: Create your own event to sell your books at. Some examples might be to partner with a local winery or brewery and sell tickets. Participants get tastings and you get to sell your books. Or you might partner with someone selling things related to your topic, such as crafting supplies or even jewelry. Theresa's cover of *Warehouse Dreams* has a hummingbird on it and she's offered books to jewelry makers who use hummingbirds.

What About Free Stuff to Get Readers?

We can sense you peeking in your pockets, wondering how much money to set aside. Writing is cheap, marketing isn't. But don't worry; there's lots of stuff you can do to sell books for free. However, the tradeoff will be your time, so choose wisely.

Social Media

Social media is either one of the best things ever created, or it's destroying our society, depending on your views. Facebook, Instagram, Twitter, and TikTok allow people to stay in contact with their friends and family, learn new things and just laugh. It's also extremely addicting (see dopamine discussion below) and can negatively affect mental health. For authors, it's also a great way to connect with potential readers. So how 'bout them apples?

Dopamine and social media algorithms

Dopamine is a hormone your brain makes. It's a pleasure hormone and can create neural pathways (paths your brain follows to link sensations, emotions, actions and thoughts together). That joyful anticipation feeling evoked by smelling the musty, cool smell of Pirates of the Caribbean at Disneyland is caused by a neural pathway. That small burst of joy when you see a text message from a loved one is caused by a neural pathway. Neural pathways can be positive or negative and are created without your consent. You can rewire your neural pathways through changing actions and being mindful of thoughts and emotions and taking actions around those, but it's difficult.[1] If you've ever heard of mindfulness activities or "rewiring" the brain, they're talking about changing neural pathways.

Anyway, back to dopamine. Dopamine is produced

whenever we do something pleasurable that our brains decide helps us to stay alive. So enjoyable food, sex, being warm, comforted, and friendship all flood our brains with dopamine, creating neural pathways. And social media triggers friendship. Getting likes, followers and views floods our brains with dopamine and keeps us wanting to go back for more and more (as Theresa just stopped what she was doing to pick up her phone to look at a Facebook notification). This means that a lot of our time and energy goes into getting that dopamine hit. Your goal as a bookseller is to become a part of your fans' dopamine. #TheDream.

Also, a word on algorithms. Algorithms are the social media programmers ways of deciding what topics viewers get. It's automated and constantly changing, but the goal is to get you to see what YOU want to see and then sell you products/ideas/classes etc. around those. That's why you often feel that everyone has the same views you do, or you never see certain people's posts. It's the algorithm choosing it for you based on what IT thinks you want. And at publication, the algorithms have gotten superb at deciding accurately what you want to see. That's why the ads you see on Instagram are specifically targeted to the things you were looking up in your browser or that you were talking to your coworkers about.

Also, also, a word on hashtags (#); hashtags, or depending on your generation, pound signs, are a way to look up various trending topics. You can use hashtags to make your post be found when other people are looking up that hashtagged word in the search bar. Your posts should almost always include trending hashtags. However, today's hashtags may get a million views, but tomorrow they may get five. Researching what hashtags work shouldn't take you more than a few minutes a day; most platforms have a trending hashtag section, which makes it super easy to find.

Remember to also only use hashtags that relate to your work or your branding, otherwise it might feel spammy to people who run across you in a bike marathon hashtag when you're selling a book about hamsters.

Your goal as a bookseller is to understand and manipulate the algorithms so your posts get seen by the people most likely to purchase your books. There are thousands, if not millions, of different strategies about this, so we're just going to brush the surface.

- If you're not already on social media, but are interested enough to try it to sell your books, choose one platform. If you're already on social media, choose the one or two platforms you're most comfortable with or spend most of your time on and find where your readers are hanging out on that platform. Use your media kit to help you determine where they might be.
- Gen Z readers are not on Facebook as Facebook tends to trend toward Gen X and Boomers. Men tend to be more on Twitter on TikTok. Do your research!
- Spend time scrolling to understand what you're seeing, and what others are trying. In Instagram and TikTok, trends are vital to your success.
- Get followers: There's two views on this.
- Get as many followers as possible. You can do this by following people, hoping they follow you back and/or by joining follow parties. The downside to this is that you may not get people who want to engage with you. However, some platforms, like TikTok provide rewards and unlock extra capabilities when you reach a certain number of followers.

- Get engaged followers. This way is much harder, but you do this by posting things that people really enjoy and they want to keep following you to learn more about.
- Engage. Don't just "like." Comment on every post of the people you would like to engage with. This does two things: it tells the platform you're using it, that you're active and that they should help your posts perform better. It also tells the human beings you're commenting on that you care about them and they should engage with you too. It's a weird, sci-fi-esk game of chess with a computer.
- Start posting... stuff. Yeah, we can hear you asking, "what kind of stuff?" Well, it varies and there's no right answer... but go back to that branding exercise and build from there!
- Buy my book posts. This is the point of you being on social media for marketing, so posting things to make people interested in your book is vital. There's some debate on how much to post about your book. Some people say to flood the market, because the algorithms will make it so few will see your posts. In this theory, the more the better. However, many view this as "spammy," so if you take this route, be aware of that perception. Others say to do the 80/20 rule; 80% on "other", 20% on book selling. Like everything, the truth is in the middle. Here are some tips on HOW to post "buy my book" posts:
- Post a link to a place to purchase your book. This is probably the least efficient, because you need a reason someone should buy your book. Also, the algorithms often make it so these posts

aren't as seen as others. It's directing people away from the social media platform. However, posting links works great if it's part of an ad you're paying for.

- Use a quote from the book. This is very effective, but you should try to combine it with marketing programs such as Canva or BookBrush to get a visually appealing post. Use still pictures or videos, but ensure you have the rights to use the photos/videos so you don't encounter any copyright issues.

- Use a snippet from the book. This works well on video montages, especially for Instagram or TikTok. You can also do the book flip. (Follow just about any Booktoker or Bookstagramer and you'll see what that means.)

- Use a snippet from a review, or screen share from an actual review, thanking the reader for the review.

- Quotes related to books or writing. Theresa finds this very effective as it's easy to go on Pinterest and just grab pre-made lovely quotes. Other writers/readers interact with them as well.

- Comments on what's going on with your life. This varies dramatically and will depend on the author brand you're portraying. You could focus only on writing and comment on what you're working on, how many edits you've done, how many words you've written, etc. Or you could comment on the weather, your pets, your kids, a leak you had in your house, a weird sunset you saw, etc. However, these posts should follow your branding. So Dennis Crosby posts a great deal about whiskey and cigars. Theresa lately is focusing on time management tips for writers, so posts her schedule or what she could get done.

- Pictures/videos from your life. Social media is primarily visual, so make sure you use lots of pictures and videos, especially on TikTok.
- Comments on something you saw/a question asked/a comment you want to make. These "confessional" posts do very well on TikTok and Instagram and you can get good engagement.
- Ask a question. This is a great way to build engagement. Theresa has had outstanding success asking others to comment on their favorite author, favorite book or favorite character.
- As we mentioned earlier, start engaging with those that engage with you.
- Like and/or comment on every comment you get on a post, unless it goes viral, and that's truly unmanageable.
- Be polite. We all enjoy those popcorn posts (meaning you're just reading the comments to see how snippy people get), but you may not want this to happen to you. It can be stressful, if not intentional, and can damage your brand and reputation. However, if you were intentionally rude to increase engagement or prove a point, then go for it!

Pro Tip: Goodreads is an EXCELLENT place to find and connect readers. Find them there, then start engaging with them. Genuine interactions show you care and that you're someone worth looking into.

A word of caution, don't get trapped in binge scrolling through social media. Swiping up can be addicting and may inhibit your creative process. Binge watching television or streaming shows can also become incredible distractions drawing you away from your writing time. If you feel super creative after or have to stop playing a video game to jot down an idea, then keep going. But if you feel empty and brain dead after video games, see if taking a break or playing less inspires your creativity. Sarah plays a variety of video games and finds that after playing (she sets about an hour limit to herself per session) she is inspired and feels ready to write. For her, playing helps her to disconnect from the troubles of the day, to totally immerse herself in something else completely unrelated to anything else. If there is something like that for you, gardening, walking, fishing, aquascaping, etc. that helps to clear your mind, do it. Find the distraction that provides a healthy, inspirational mind-space for you.

There is a great deal of debate about the effects of social media on mental health. Some say it's a great way to escape for a little while, but, a we've cautioned earlier, the mindless scrolling of social media can also have a detrimental factor to your creativity (it can also cost you time, but more on that in a later chapter). Many of us do what Joanna Penn from the Creative Penn Podcast calls, "doom scrolling," seeing social media posts that cause fear and anxiety. Doom scrolling can have a huge effect on your creativity. A recent study by the University of Bath recommends taking week long hiatuses from social media will actually, "lead to significant improvements in their wellbeing, depression and anxiety and could, in the future, be recommended as a way to help people manage their mental health…"[2] Daily use of social media over-stimulates and tires out our brains. However, creating social media using visual platforms like TikTok and Instagram can also improve your creativity and help you see things a little differently. So in conclusion… yeah… we don't know either. Do social media to help with marketing, but be careful with your mental health and overall wellbeing.

Exercise (20 minutes): Social Media

It's time to think about social media.

- Do you plan to use social media? If so, do you plan to use your own accounts or create new ones that are only for your author life?
- Which platforms do you want to use? How familiar are you with the platform?
- How much time do you want to devote to this on a daily/weekly/monthly basis? Remember, social media is addicting, so consider setting limits.
- Do you have time or the desire to spend learning social media platforms or do you want to just "wing it?" (No wrong answer by the way–it's just which strategy do you want to use?)
- Will you use any time saving platforms for posting such as Hootsuite or Canva?
- Do you want to just post when you feel like it, or do you want to pre-plan your posts?

- Do you want to hire someone or ask a family
  member/friend to help with your social media?

Pro Tip: Social media is a PART of marketing, it does not
nor should it encompass all of it. Marketing includes:
author branding, reaching out to the media, having a newsletter, networking, and yes, posting pictures of the cup of
coffee that you spilled on your notes for your latest book.
All these pieces help to build awareness of who we are (yes,
that's important), and of the books we write. That way,
when people start to like you and the more and more they
see your name (BUT for the love of writing, please don't
spam them), they'll be more likely to pick up your book at
the store and think, hunh, why is this name familiar?

The key to social media is to commit to it and do it regularly
for at least 6 months to keep momentum going. Get that
inertia going and keep it rolling. The more that ball starts
rolling down the hill, the more it's going to gather and the
faster it's going to go.

Interviews

Interviews are a great and free way to get your name and
books in front of others and there are tons of opportunities
for writers. The easiest are the newsletter interviews where

you answer a bunch of questions in advance and in writing, and that interview is placed in a newsletter, on someone's blog, or on their social media. If you have a newsletter, this is a great way to increase your subscribers.

Then there're magazines, YouTube, Facebook Live, or blog interviews, which are similar, but may want to interview you in person, over the phone or via an online video platform. Podcast, radio and television interviews are the same format and require you to be in person, but thanks to Zoom, the possibilities of these platforms have exploded. Most of these are pre-recorded, but not all, so take the time to understand the parameters. There's nothing worse than doing your hair and make-up thinking the interview will be on YouTube, but it's only an audio recording. Or the opposite where you feel comfy in your sweats and hairband, but you're appearing on Facebook Live.

Don't sit back and wait for someone to message you for an interview, especially if you're a fiction writer; they may not until you're "famous." Send out requests for interviews. Theresa has a quick message she sends consisting of:

> "Hello (person),
>
> My name is Theresa Halvorsen and I'm a speculative fiction writer of works such as Warehouse Dreams and River City Widows, besides various short stories. I'm also the co-owner and chief editor at No Bad Books Press, LCC and a co-host with Semi-Sages of the Pages. I enjoyed your podcast... because... And it helped me realize... My website is www.theresahauthor.com so you can learn more about me. Thanks for your time and I look forward to hearing from you soon."

Theresa has also had brilliant success finding podcasts to interview her by hanging out on social media. When someone mentions a podcast interviewed them, she reaches out to that podcast to see if they're interested in interviewing her. Many podcasts also put out "calls" on social media asking for interviewees. You can also ask on your social media if anyone knows of any podcasts interviewing. Then there's also a Google search for podcasts in your genre. If nothing else, you may find a good professional development podcast.

However, it's very important you do your research prior to reaching out to them. Know what the podcast/magazine/blog is about. Plan to listen to an episode or two (at least) or read some of the back posts/magazines. When your interview comes out, make sure you mention it in your newsletter, website and social media. They're interviewing you, trying to expand their reach. It's polite to help them out and will help you get more interviews in the future.

So what do you talk about in your interviews? Go back once again to that author branding kit. Remember those three to five articles you wrote? Use those as talking points and/or ways to connect to the interviewer's audience. Look for niche podcasts that relate to your branding or book–they're out there! And don't poo-poo a podcast if it has a few listeners. Some authors have found hundreds of readers after being on small podcasts with a voracious fanbase.

Book Clubs

Book clubs are fantastic places to approach about your book, especially if it's a fiction book or a memoir. Some book clubs want nothing more than just to read your books, while others will want to do an interview or invite you to their club if you're local. Like with interviews, there's no harm in asking.

Finding book clubs can be tricky though. Our tips for this are:

- Look for local clubs on Facebook, NextDoor, MeetUp, etc. and reach out to them similar to how you would for an interview.
- Post on your website that you're available to chat at book clubs.
- Have a list of book club topics about your book on your website. Heck, if you can, include it within your book!
- And of course, check in with your local library and see if they have a book club within your genre.

Pro Tip: Start your own book club and invite your author friends to speak at it. See if your author friends will do the same for you.

Write Professional Articles/Short stories:

If you're a nonfiction writer, it's mandatory to write lots of nonfiction articles in various places about your topic. Include your newsletter sign-ups in your bio or tag line! Doing this will help you find your audience before your book comes out. You can ask to be a guest contributor by querying various blogs and magazines—and many will pay you for your expertise and time. Medium is also a great place to publish your articles; payment consists of page reads. You should also have a blog on your website you can steer your fans to.

If you're a fiction writer, short stories/anthologies are a great way to get your name in front of new fans. However, you will have to query for these, which can be time-consuming. The rejection rate is also very high; there are more people querying than places to put all the short stories. The Semi-Sages of the Pages actually host a "Race for the Rejection" channel on our Discord channel to help people keep querying. We celebrate rejections because it means you're actually out there trying to get your works published.

If you're a fiction writer, you can also write articles on writing and world building, and submit to various publications, including Medium, which is a great way to get seen (and maybe paid).

Panels

With COVID-19, many conventions with panels went virtual or will have a virtual platform. Panels are a great way to meet other writers, and get in front of new readers. And like with interviewing, it's easy to get on them; just ask. It helps if you have a more experienced buddy who already has a panel at an event. You can either jump on with them or have access to the panel planner to whom you can suggest a panel.

Places to find panels include bookstores, libraries and conventions. If you're a nonfiction writer, trade conventions specific to your topics are vital. For fiction writers; those various comic or romance conventions are great places to speak about your characters and world building, even if you're not a speculative or romance fiction writer.

Book Signings

Be honest… when many of you thought about being an author, there was an element of opening your book, writing some catch phrase, signing it and handing it to some adoring fan, right? (It's also totally ok if that's not your vision.) Book signings are often paired with lectures, panels, events, and conventions. The exception to this are book signings at bookstores, but those can be challenging to get as you're just starting out. Additionally, book signings may not be free; you may have to purchase and bring your own books, and there may be additional fees.

In Conclusion about the Free Stuff

Wow, it's taken us a while to get here and we're just scraping the surface. You can go more in depth on all the topics above with a Google or YouTube search if interested. All the above ideas can be effective ways to market and find new readers, but they can be time-consuming, may not work or may not appear to work. There's an adage that says it takes someone seeing a product seven to ten times before they purchase it. This is the goal of using free platforms. You're trying to get people to see your book everywhere, so they're interested in purchasing it.

As mentioned in the beginning, all of these have a time element, so please balance your time and money. One you can always get more of; the other you can't.

Speaking in Front of Others

Another thing we wanted to address are those of you who have anxiety with the idea of public speaking, sitting on panels or taking part in events. It's ok not to do this stuff. You can still sell books with none of this. But if you'd like to stretch and become more comfortable speaking in front of others, here are some tips.

- Time to pull out that brand you created. It's not YOU on that panel, it's your brand. Being your brand is a form of acting, a form of pretending, of picking a persona rather than YOU.
- It's also ok if you're awkward. Everyone has awkward moments, everyone has times when they wish they could take something back, everyone has those moments when they don't know what to say, everyone has those moments when they speak for far too long, (like this sentence). Embrace it! People will understand. And if they don't… you don't want to sell them your book, anyway.
- Practice, practice, practice. Imagine what it would be like, imagine your answers and what you would say, imagine people clapping and clamoring in adoration for you (if that helps).
- Practice with a friend. It's silly, but it truly helps if you practice your answers, your smiles and even your book signing signature with a friend.
- Zoom or Teams interviews may be easier to start with, as you can focus on yourself and not on the interviewer.
- Go with a friend. It helps if you have someone who can tell you, you're going to do amazing,

and then can tell you how amazing you were afterwards.

- Choose a friendly crowd. When Theresa did her first television interview, she was petrified, but the anchor was very kind. He told her to breathe and that she'd do great under his breath as the camera panned to her. It also helps if you have a friend in the crowd you can focus on as you speak.
- Hire someone to help you. There are coaches out there that can help you get past anxiety and give you some tips on getting up on that stage or talking to others.

Exercise (10 minutes): Choosing the free stuff

Now's the time to pull out your goals and your branding again. If you're a quiet person who doesn't enjoy interacting with others, then events and book signings may not be worth it. Ditto with podcast interviews. But take some time to decide what free stuff you want to pursue. Make a list of five items from the above sections as a launching point to build from later.

Places to Sell your Books

Don't forget, there are more options other than just selling your books online.

Book Stores

If you're a lover of books, which we assume you are, you know that there's something magical about walking into a bookstore. Whether you're an indie or traditionally published author, bookstores can be an incredibly valuable part of your marketing plan. However, even traditionally published authors may not get into bookstores automatically. If you're traditionally published, with a marketing team behind you, check with them before you go into a bookstore to see if they'd be interested in stocking your book. Your publisher may have a distribution deal that is already in the works for this or they may appreciate the help.

But if you're an indie author, it's best to go into the bookstores, with a copy of your book (do not give to them) and your sell sheet. A sell sheet is a one-page document consisting of the following:

- The name of the book
- The cover
- Your name and a brief bio
- A brief summary (the blurb is fine)
- The word count
- Where they can purchase your book (if you're indie, this is IngramSpark, if you're with a publisher, ask your publisher). Please note, bookstores do not want to purchase from Amazon. If you want your book to be in bookstores, you need to publish in IngramSpark.

Develop a relationship with the bookstores you're after. Don't just go in and be like, "Hi, my name is... Would you like to sell my book?" Talk to the booksellers, get to know them, get to know their audience. If you're approaching a store that only sells science fiction and fantasy, but you're a Jane Austen-style contemporary romance novelist, you're not the best fit for them. Do your research. If you find one that is a good fit, offer to give a presentation in their shop so that you are bringing people to the bookstore. You're building a relationship with the booksellers and it has to benefit both parties.

Tenacity is the key; you may have to try several times before they stock your book on the shelves. And to keep it there, tell your fans so they go to purchase it from their local bookshop. Or encourage them to ask their book-keepers to cary your tales in their shops. If enough people ask, the book carriers will be far more willing to carry a product that's in demand.

Gift Shops and Boutiques

If you've a nonfiction book or a fiction book with a local location or a local historically significant character, gift shops can be great places to sell your books. Just like with bookstores, be prepared to go in with your sell sheet and a copy of your book. On the plus side, the gift store might purchase the books on consignment, rather than through a distributor, which means you get paid if the book sells. If you're a children's book author, children's stores are great places to approach.

six

but there's only 24-hours in a day– how do you do all of this?

> "You may delay, but time will not."
> *-Benjamin Franklin*

AH! This is about time management.

By now, you've learned that being a successful author is about a lot more than just writing brilliant words and creating memorable dialogue and worlds. Most authors start out having dual, triple or quadruple lives, including day jobs, family lives, elderly parents, a partner, friends and/or young children. So if you're looking around wondering where-on-earth you'll find the time to have this writing life, remember, the time will pass anyway. Don't look back and regret not finding that hour, that thirty minutes a day for your dream.

But finding the time is going to take some planning, some reflection and some choices.

In *The Writing Life*, Annie Dillard says, "how we spend our days is, of course, how we spend our lives. What we do with this hour, and that one, is what we are doing."

Or another way to put this,

"When you say yes to something, you say no to something else."

So if you're all in, but saying, "I really and truly don't have the time," we're here to help. You have more time than you realize!

Exercise (20 minutes): Spending Time

How do you spend your non-writing (including marketing) time? Don't think, just list.

- Chores? What specifically?
- Friends? Who? (This includes friends you don't see, but only call, text or chat online with.)
- Family time?
- Social media?
- TV/movies/books/entertainment? (This includes things like concerts and sporting events.)
- A job?
- School/learning/online classes?
- Hobbies?
- Sleep?
- Exercise?
- Eating? (This includes eating out)
- Self care? (However you define it)
- Commute/taking kids to school or classes?
- Doctors/Dentist/medical appointments? (this includes those you attend for other people)

If you're like Theresa and you say, "but I find writing time in the middle of these," that's ok, just list them out anyway. Consider it bonus time at this point of the chapter. And if you're wondering how on earth you can find writing time while doing these, we've got you!

Now take that list and try to figure out how much time,

either minutes or daily percentage you spend on those things. There will be some overlap, but try to figure out your priorities. And no one other than you is going to see this list, so don't create an ideal list that says you spend no time watching TV, but you've watched *For All Mankind* three times last month.

Now answer the following questions:

- What are you willing to give up? If not willing to give up entirely, what are you willing to reduce? Go into detail and take some time to reflect as you go through your daily life.
- If you're reducing your chores, which ones? Are you willing to wash your car every other week instead of every other?
- If you're cutting back on family/friend time, how are they going to react to this?
- Are there things you can combine? Hiking, for example, may take care of spending time with friends, self-care, hobbies, and exercise, but going to the gym may not.
- What are you willing to let others do for you? Are you willing to pay others for this? Think more than just a maid: think of gardeners, dog-walkers, a teenager to hang with your kids and help with homework, using a shopping service like Instacart, using a service like Amazon for those annoying, "I forgot to gets," offering a few bucks to your teenager to help with social media, etc.
- Do you have any money you can put toward time management, apps or delivery fees that can help? Can you even afford a gardener, for example?

This exercise will help you target areas where you can find time. We highly recommend having a frank talk with your family, especially if you primarily do the chores/errands/driving the kids around, etc. You can't do it all, and if you're going to let some of it go, you're going to need their help to be successful and to find balance. It might be hard, but ask them to respect your writing time. Those ten minutes, two hours where you just need to be left alone in your zone to write, that is your sacred time for you and the world you are building. There are always exceptions to this rule, but have that talk with your family expressing how important this is to you. In an interview with Sarah, author K.A. Fox described how she had that talk with her family a few years ago, and now her children will heckle her if she's procrastinating, saying things to her like, "Mom, shouldn't you be writing?" And she loves it. Their heckling isn't an annoyance, it's their way of supporting their mom in pursuing her dream. There's something really quite special about that.

Theresa: *My husband took on grocery shopping and cooking (which I hate anyways). He also attempts to have dinner ready close to when I get home to free up as much evening time as possible. It also helps that he runs his own business and understands those demands. He will never ask for my attention if I can't give it. And I'll do the same for him.*

Sarah: *I wouldn't be where I am in my writing career without my Salvatore. He cooks dinner even though he's not a fan of cooking. He makes the coffee every morning and does a lot of the laundry. These tasks might seem like little things in the grand scheme, but these chores take A LOT of time. I am grateful to him for all that he does to support my dreams, especially his respecting my writing time when I go into my office to write/edit/cover design, when I* *know he'd rather (and I'd rather) be curled up watching TV with him. Respecting the foundations of their relationship is one of my HUGE priorities. It took time for us to find balance, but it is worth taking the time to figure out with your loved ones together.*

List Making

"Just for today, I will have a program. I might not follow it exactly, but I will have it. I will save myself from two enemies—hurry and indecision."
-Frank Crane

Upon Sarah's grandma Faxon's bedroom wall hung a frame with eight hand written "just for todays." One of the just for todays was the quote above by Frank Crane and it's one Sarah pays particular attention to almost every day. As a result of grandma's wisdom, Sarah has long been an avid fan of lists.

Yeah, we heard that groan. But we believe list making is an important way to maximize your time and help you stay organized. Here are a few ways to experiment with the process to make it work for you. And just like with every-thing else, what works for you may not work for another and vice versa.

- Info dump: Just put it all down on paper. Dump everything in your mind onto one place. From an organizational perspective, it's not the best, but it feels good to get it out of your head and onto a piece of paper, into your phone, or scribbled on a tablet.

- Create lists based on need or project. Apps like Trello can help you with this. For example, Theresa's weekend lists may look like this:
- Vacation planning
- Buy a new bathing suit
- Schedule pedicure
- Buy snacks for the plane trip
- House stuff
- Vacuum fans
- Wash couch blankets (don't judge... her dogs sleep on those)
- Organize under bathroom sink
- Writing stuff
- Write two Vella chapters
- Outline next phase of Warehouse world
- NBBP Business
- Update ten ads
- Inventory count after Saturday event
- Order more postcards for next event
- Go into the details on your lists. This can help prevent feeling overwhelmed by a gigantic task, like "update website". Instead, you would write:
- Update bio section of website
- Announce next book
- Update event section of website
- Change header pictures
- Organize based on prioritization. There are nuances to this that many people swear by. Some people take that info dump list and split it into quarters using the Eisenhower Matrix or the Stephen Covey Quad Chart to help you find out what you HAVE to do vs what you NEED to do.

	Urgent	Not Urgent
Important		
Not Important		

The Eisenhower Matrix

If you'd like to really dive deep into ways to become more productive, Chris Bailey, author of *The Productivity Project*, details several various strategies based on his personal experiences and countless hours of research. One trick he recommends that both Theresa and Sarah adhere to is setting three MUST DOs every day and then prioritizing them.

Theresa has created her own quad chart and splits her boxes into:

1. Must Do (things that are under a deadline)
2. Should Do (things that keep the ball rolling)
3. Want to Do (fun things or interesting research)
4. Let it Go or Will Get to, if have Time
   (everything else)

Another tactic that Sarah uses from Bailey, is to number

her list based on priority. Number one is almost always the thing she wants to do least. That way, she's "swallowed that frog" and won't have to worry about that one thing for the rest of her day.

Exercise (15 minutes): Start That List!

1. Make a list of everything that's on your mind.
2. Prioritize it using any of the above tactics.
3. Start checking a few things off your "Must Dos".
4. See if you can get to your "Should Dos".

Creating Schedules

Another time management trick involves scheduling time to create more. This can help when you make your list and then prioritize it. So a sample schedule might look like this (ok, this is actually Theresa's).

Weekdays:

- 4:30 A.M.: Wake up
- 4:30 A.M.–5:15 A.M.: Shower, make-up, getting dressed etc.
- 5:15 A.M.–6:00 A.M.: Breakfast, lunch prep and 30 minutes of editing
- 6:00 A.M.–6:10: Final prep before leaving
- 6:10 A.M.–7:05 A.M.: Commute
- 7:05 A.M.–4:30ish P.M.: Work
- 4:30 P.M.–5:30 P.M.: Commute
- 5:45 P.M. (buffer time built in)–6:45 P.M.: Dinner, dog walk, exercise and/or meeting/interview, etc.
- 7:00 P.M. (buffer time built-in)–9:00 P.M.: Writing (if meetings haven't run into this time)

- 9:00 P.M.–10:00 P.M.: Time with hubby/social media/Amazon Ads/admin tasks updates
- 10:15 P.M./10:30 P.M. (buffer time built in): Bed

Weekends:

- 6:30 A.M.: Wake up
- 6:30 A.M.–7:00 A.M.: Social media/Amazon ads/wake-up (Theresa needs a lot of caffeine before she can function and does social media and Amazon ads* until she's awake)
- 7:00 A.M.–8:30 A.M.: Edit *Gods at Play* by Gregory Hughes
- 8:30 A.M.–9:00A.M.: Dog walk/exercise
- 9:00 A.M.–10:00 A.M.: Breakfast/shower/chores/get ready for day
- 10:00 A.M.–1:00 P.M.: Chores/errand running
- 1:00 P.M.–2:00 P.M.: Work on *Tiny Gateways*
- 2:00 P.M.–3:30 P.M.: Edit *Transcendence of Marciana* by Izabela Markus
- 3:30 P.M.–4:00 P.M.: Break/buffer time/reflection/mental health check-in
- 4:00 P.M.–5:00 P.M.: Social media/NBBP stuff
- 5:00 P.M.–10:00 P.M.: Time with friends/family/husband/non-writing hobbies (does that exist?)

If you have lots to do, set time limits on it so you can try to accomplish many things, rather than just getting sucked into one thing.

Theresa: *Fun Amazon ads story about what not to do. Because I need a great deal of caffeine to wake up, I accidentally set up an Amazon ad with a keyword that cost $2.00/click rather than the*

40-50 cents I normally run my ads at. I caught it, but not before the ad had run for several days and was wondering why the ads were costing so much more. Also, because the keyword was $2.00/click instead of cheaper, it got lots of clicks, which cost more money than I wanted to spend. So... don't do things that involve attention to detail if you're still waking up.

Exercise (20 minutes): Building a Schedule

On a free weekend, try building a schedule. Start with the things you HAVE to do, especially if they have times associated with it, such as taking the kids to a soccer game. Then figure out the things you HAVE to do, but don't have a time frame around. Think grocery shopping, mowing the lawn or getting that oil change. Add those to your schedule. Then add the things you WANT to do, or the things that have a deadline, but it's not immediate. Don't forget to factor in time with your family/friends. And if you work a day job, you may need the weekends to recoup—don't over-book yourself or you'll burn out.

Setting Aside a Certain Number of Hours a Week/Month

Another technique you can use is setting aside a certain number of hours in a week for certain tasks. This one takes a lot of discipline so you don't go over and rob time away from another task, but many find it effective. So if we assume there's 168 hours in a week, your allocation might look like this:

- Sleep: 49 hours (7 hours a night)
- Eating/prepping food: 14 hours (2 hours a day)[1]
- Exercise: 3.5 hours a week (30 minutes a day)
- Grooming: 7 hours (1 hour a day)

- Writing: 35 hours (5 hours a day)
- Marketing: 20 hours (4 hours a day)
- Self-care/mental health: 7 hours (1 hour a day)
- Family/friend/pet time: 14 hours (2 hours a day)
- Chores/Errands etc: 14 hours (2 hour a day)
- Buffer: 4.5 hours

Time Management and Kids

It's difficult to plan your life and have schedules when you have kids. All it takes is one odd fever, and you've lost your entire writing time taking your child to Urgent Care. Or the time your three-year-old locked you out of the house when you went to take out the trash (happened to Theresa). Or the time you thought your kids were napping, and it turned out they'd found a sharpie pen. And decorated each other. And the walls. And the sheets. Pretty much everything within reach had sharpie ink on it (true story!). But here are some tips you can try:

- Consider paying a teenager you trust to come over and watch the kids so you can concentrate. Or ask a friend to watch them for you. But you have to hide. Lock yourself in a closet or the bathroom where they can't interrupt you. Or better yet, find a coffee shop to hang out in.
- Use those kid's activities to your advantage. Rather than dropping the kids off, then going home, loading the dishwasher and taking out the trash, then going back to the activity for pickup, stay where you're at. Work in your car or find a coffee shop. Theresa found she was super focused and able to get a ton done during those times.

- Consolidate everything! Finding those pockets of time is invaluable. So plan your grocery store/Target/Walmart runs, so it's only once a week. Set up those automatic deliveries from Amazon so you don't run out of paper towels and have to drop everything to run to the store because your dog peed on the floor. Don't take your kids with you on those errands so you can move fast (and you'll save money because they won't add random things to the cart).
- Meal prep. Take some time and plan out lunches, breakfast and meals so they're fast, affordable and take as little time as possible. But be careful of spending too much time organizing your fridge and pantry. That organization can end up costing you more time than saving. Find the balance.
- Write wherever you can. We know an author whose child was having some problems falling asleep, so she would write while sitting outside his door on the floor. She was still available if he needed her, but she could get some work done.
- You'd be amazed how many people will help you, if you ask. Ask for carpool help, shopping help and meal prep help. Offer to make a double batch of something and ask for the favor to be returned. Pay your teenager to help around the house so you can concentrate. And have that talk with your partner about what you can and can't truly do.
- Many parents write after their kids are asleep, and while this is great, it may not be sustainable in the long term, and may affect your mental

health. Be careful trading sleep for writing time (*Theresa: I feel judged, but also agree*).

- Multi-tasking healthily. When exercising and doing chores, listen to those podcasts on professional development. When in the car driving between places, call your mom for a check-in. Make friends with other authors; that way you get friend time and professional development time.

- Learn to say no. You may find you can't be the costume coordinator for the play at the high school. You may have to miss that girls' night with those parents you really didn't like. You may have to let your partner take the kids to the park so you can concentrate. You may not be able to spend hours creating the perfect cupcakes for your child's birthday party. Look around and decide what you'll say yes to and what you can let go.

Finding Pockets of Time

We can hear you saying, "There's only 24 hours in every day and every minute is taken up! Where am I going to find pockets of time?"

If you look around, you'll find you waste a lot of time. How many times did you run up and down the stairs because you forgot something you needed?

Theresa: *This habit took me discipline to get rid of. I realized I'd lost writing time one weekend and was trying to figure out where it went. Then, I realized I'd spent thirty minutes doing the following:*

- Forgot headphones downstairs

- Wanted a cup of tea
- Lost time to TikTok waiting for tea to warm (and then it cooled)
- Let dogs out
- Kept checking TikTok
- Let dogs back in
- Got a snack
- Went upstairs to work
- Realized headphones were still downstairs

So if you look around, there are plenty of places you can find five minutes here and there to dedicate toward your passion. We understand you may not implement all of these tricks into your life, but here are some ideas to help you try to figure out ways to streamline you to having more writing time:

- Wake up ten minutes earlier (get rid of snooze— seriously, you'll feel better!).
- Take a shorter shower. Theresa now sets an alarm, so she gets out of the shower after ten minutes.
- Watch how the traffic moves during your commute. Is there a lane that moves better than others? Find it and save yourself five minutes in your commute, but *please* drive safely!
- If possible, change your work hours. If you leave ten minutes earlier, does that save you twenty minutes on your commute?
- Can you find a coffee shop before or after your job to decrease your commute? So rather than jumping in the car at 5:00 P.M. and spending ninety minutes in traffic, can you spend an hour

in a coffee shop, and decrease your commute to
forty-five minutes?[2]

- Reorganize your spaces
- Organize your clothes by function or color so
  you're not wasting time searching.
- Put cleaning supplies in every bathroom and in
  the kitchen.
- Put stuff that belongs upstairs on the bottom of
  the stairs for your kids to put away (and watch
  your kids step over them)
- Organize the makeup products you use on a day-
  to-day basis or put your make-up in a bag you
  pull out every morning, rather than digging
  through a drawer.
- Put a fridge with drinks in your workspace.
- Put things away the first time so you don't have
  to search for it.
- Organize your virtual life
- Name articles, posts you want to keep the same
  way and save them in a special folder or print
  them out so you can find them.
- Use the search function in Outlook or Gmail so
  you can find emails easily.
- Take a class on Outlook organization.
- Race through your chores. Theresa puts a time
  limit on chores and competes against herself to
  see how fast she can complete them.
- Delegate chores. Have a list of chores for
  everyone in your house so one person doesn't
  have to do everything.
- Automate everything! Got an invite for a
  concert? When Google asks if you want to add it
  to your calendar, say yes! Love that make-up?
  Agree to have it come monthly so you don't have

to go to the store once a month only to find out that product isn't in stock. (Side note: this is not a book on saving money, we're talking about time management and that can get expensive.)

- Use text to voice features for important reminders so you don't forget something.
- Carry professional materials with you. The best schedule in the world can't prevent an airplane crashing on the freeway in front of you (true story) causing you to be three hours late for a party. If you have professional materials with you, you can work while you're stuck in traffic rather than complaining to everyone in the car about how much time you're wasting. If you're the one driving, have an app on your phone that records your voice so you can audibly take notes.
- Write on your lunch breaks. Sarah used to bring her iPad and or a notebook with her to her day jobs and would write away while eating. It may feel insane (it may look insane), but squeezing in those 15-20 minutes on your lunch break can add up quickly.

Be cautious with this mentality though. Depending on your personality, trying to count every moment may not work for you. It may limit your creativity or decrease your mental health (or distract you from paying attention while you're driving). It can also add stress that YOU'VE put on yourself. When you're paying attention to every moment, there's nothing worse than giving yourself thirty minutes to vacuum and then finding out you have to take apart the vacuum, eating up those thirty minutes and pushing the rest of your schedule back. It's stressful if you don't remember these are deadlines and schedules you've placed on yourself.

If you can't think like this, or find trying to find pockets of time stressful, then that's fine. Don't do it.

Exercise (15 minutes): Finding Pockets of Time

Spend a few days paying attention to the times you race up and down the stairs, or stand by the backdoor scrolling through social media. Notice the amount of time you spend digging through cabinets for a spice or a tool in a toolbox. How much time do you spend trying to find an email? Those times you hit snooze. The time you spend in the shower. Notice the times you say, "this is a waste of time."

Decide if you can trim back/remove any of that time. Start small or you won't maintain it.

Bonus: Continue to assess for a full month, and see how many pockets of time you can find.

A word about Multi-Tasking

You can't do it. No, you can't. Truly. It's actually pretty bad for your mental health.[3] What you're doing is jumping back and forth between tasks. It's not healthy and leads to mental health challenges. It also increases mistakes and does not save you any time. Instead, it creates an adrenaline feed-back loop that tricks you into thinking you're completing more than you would. But you're not. That adrenaline is also addicting.

Theresa: Whenever I fall into one of these cycles, I tell myself to "line them up and knock them down." Meaning grab a problem or task, complete it, then move on to the next. It's actually very calming when you're feeling like there's too much to do and ALL of it is a priority.

Also, if part of your multitasking comprises checking social media without intention, you are not multitasking.

You're feeding that dopamine you're addicted to and not actually working, even if you tell yourself you're "marketing." (Theresa, guilty of this, hangs head in shame.)

When you're writing, think about your story and only that. Don't have three balls in the air at a time. After all, your characters will get jealous if you're fixated on your weekend plans when you should be hanging out with them.

The Need for Reflection and Procrastination

Human beings need time to reflect, and as Stephen King says, let the boys in the basement do their thing. This is why staring into a fire, at ocean waves or into a fish tank feels so peaceful. Or perhaps you've seen the videos that show paint pouring or fingers running through play-dough. Have you ever watched one of those, felt better, and then known how to solve a writing or plot problem you had? Or after watching one, were you able to bang out a thousand words? You needed that time to let your conscious brain rest, while your subconscious and unconscious kept going.

Procrastination is often seen as a bad thing, and if we're talking about time management, many will focus on eliminating it. Procrastination is often a way for your subconscious to work while your consciousness does something else. You need to reset and restore or you'll find your creativity taking a hit. You just have to figure out a balance to make it work for you.

So if you know you need to write that chapter, but find the slight glaze of dust across your books distracting and you really want to go clean it, you're procrastinating. We recommend taking a moment to assess why you're procrastinating. Is the task something you don't want to do? Why? Is the task hard or you don't know how to get it done, like that plot hole you discovered in chapter five that destroys your climatic ending? Rather than forcing yourself to fix that problem, could you do something different? Talk it over with a friend? Do some brain mapping, or some art about it? What is it that's blocking you from checking it off your list?

Finally, if you really and truly can't focus on something, move on to something else. Some find finishing difficult tasks impossible, and if that's you, it's ok. Don't beat yourself up. Don't waste your valuable time trying to milk something your brain won't let you do. Take a break, or go onto your next project. But then that takes us into the problem of idea fairying.

Idea Fairying

"Idea fairying" is a concept Theresa learned about from a leader at a department meeting. They were discussing a problem, and it was one of those vivacious meetings where everyone is shouting ideas, and building off each other. And after Theresa added idea number one million to the ridiculous and impractical list, her boss looked at her and said, "I need fewer idea fairies and more people who will actually get the job done."

Ouch.

But her boss' frustration was valid. Idea fairying or the act of coming up with ideas and layering them on top of others is so much freaking fun! That adrenaline, that burst of creativity, that moment of energy when you get an amazing idea and can't wait to get it out on paper, to run with it, to create it, to birth it into the world. It's truly one of the most incredible feelings for creatives.

The problem, from a time management perspective, is that you can fall into a trap of uncompleted projects. Because idea fairying feels so good, but finishing a project is so freaking hard, you can end up with a million half-completed ideas that just "fizzle out." We would challenge you that if they didn't fizzle out, they got hard and then you moved on to the next idea because it energized you.

So while moving onto a new project can be a way to improve your mental health and temporarily increase your focus, from the perspective of completing tasks, it may pull you away from your primary objectives. So if you fall into this trap, here are a few ideas:

- Create a place for these ideas. Theresa has no problem coming up with ideas, but lacks the time to complete them all. So she keeps a Google Docs file simply labeled "Ideas." If the idea keeps occurring to her after she's written it down, it goes up on her priority list.
- If an idea won't leave you alone, DECIDE if you want to give it some time. Look at your other projects and decide which one you will stop or slow down to give this one priority.
- If you can't give up a project or slow one down, you'll have to give up something else. Do you want to give up sleep, family time or even a few days of your day job so you can focus on this idea? Be intentional with your time!
- Can you plot it out and then give it a break? Theresa recently has been using this tactic of creating a full plot for a story, planning to write it at a future date. That way the idea doesn't disappear, and she's got the hard part, plotting, out of the way when feeling the burst from the idea fairy.

- If you're still not sure, talk it out with a blunt, practical friend. (Sarah tends to be that person — we all know at least one.)

Exercise (20 minutes): Projects

Look around. How many half-completed projects do you have? Do you find difficulty completing projects? If so, you may be an idea fairyer. Consider choosing just one of those projects and refusing to start any more until that one is complete.

Sarah: *I find that I tend to be the person who poo-poos idea fairying; I once had a job where people shot out ideas like shrapnel. I quickly found that I was the only person to pull up the e-brake and say, "So logistically, how do we do this? How will we pay for this? I think this is a good idea, but let's table it and return to the subject at hand." This isn't to say I don't get caught up in ideas, but being that person so early in my career has helped me to be that person to myself with my own projects.*

Do you have Time for Anything else?

No. Just kidding… sorta. Becoming a successful author is like starting any other small business. It takes time, but there are only 24-hours in a day and life is about living. Here are some of the other things we do when we're not writing:

Theresa: *I do have time for fun—I'm just very intentional with it. I'd rather go to a concert or a convention or spend time with my friends and family than watching streaming shows or playing video games. I miss those things, but to me, I will not look back on* *my life and wish I'd spent more time on them. Instead, I'm going to remember the vacations (Cancun and seeing Dave Mathews on a beach for three nights in a row), the crazy stories (the time one of my boys flipped the kitchen table during a game of Munchkin), the laugher (the time a neighbor yelled at us to shut up during Monty Python Flex —there was singing involved), and even the frustrating times (the time I lost it on one of my teenagers in Hawaii because I was tired, jet-lagged, and starving). Those are the moments I want to fill my free time with (well, not the yelling). That doesn't mean I don't watch streaming shows–I am a geek girl and there's lots of awesome geeky shows —I just combine it with my social media or marketing time.*

Sarah: *I have to be strategic. I've found hobbies that are accessible, don't take a lot of maintenance, but need daily attention. I have terrariums and planted aquariums, which help me disconnect and reset, but they all take less than a half hour of my attention a day. I've literally been asked if I have a time turner or a flux capacitor; let me assure you, I do not. The rules of 24 hours in a day do indeed apply to me. I just rarely indulge in binge watching shows, (you better believe I did binge watch Stranger Things and Obi-Wan), but because I make my lists and plan out my following day the night before, I'm generally very good at staying focused and checking off my tasks one item at a time. Would I prefer to be playing Zelda or scrolling through Reels? Sometimes heck-yeah I would, but I constantly remind myself this dream is worth the hard work. There are days when I don't wanna, but those are the days when I make myself work harder. It's the days, and they are rare, but they happen, when I can't that I let myself get lost in a video game because I need a mental break. Figuring out your "I cants" vs the "I don't wannas" is so important. We've said it before, but it bears saying again, you cannot forget or dismiss your mental health.*

Is it hard? Yes. Is it demanding, grueling, back-breaking and whatever other synonym you have for hard? Yes. I work a stressful fifty-hour-a week job and have a two-hour commute every day plus this writing life. Sometimes it sucks to start Saturday mornings planning out my tasks, but as I've mentioned, I adore every moment of this writing life I've chosen. I'm so incredibly grateful the stars aligned, and I can do this.

seven
but how do you become a successful author?

"I've been writing about measurement a lot this year, because I've found that measuring progress is the only way to drive lasting success."
-John Lanchester

WE'VE BEEN ASKED if there's a secret formula one can take to become successful at this writing life. And the answer is, we wish there was. The closest we've come is taking a big dose of tenacity every morning. You have to be passionate; you have to be strong; you have to be ok with falling apart, with watching plans wither and with receiving negative reviews. We all do. If there's a secret, it's to not give up on your dreams. Fairy tale-esk as that sounds, it's true. Don't give up. Humans and what we're capable of is kinda amazing. Don't forget that building a world on paper is kinda amazing too.

So we wanted to take this section to talk about the side of writing no one wants to talk about; the setbacks and the moments when you feel like giving up. Staying tough and fighting through that noise is how you will become a successful author.

Negative Reviews

Picture it, (if you read that with Sophia Petrillo's voice from *The Golden Girls*, you made Sarah's day), you've just received a notification from Goodreads that there's a new review on your book. The butterflies burst to life in your stomach as you click through the links to see what this amazing reader left for you as reviews are HARD to get. But then, you see it.

One. Gold. Star.

And, what's worse, beneath it, a scathing review. This person hated your book. They say if they could have given you zero stars they would have.

The world crumbles around you and you decide that you'll never make it as an author, and that your writing career is done.

Whoa-nelly, let's rein that negative spiral right on back. One star, two star, three star reviews are going to happen. Our books are art and, like art, how someone reacts to it is subjective and different for every person. Before you start to psychoanalyze the individual who left you that one star, walk away.

That's right, walk away. Do something else. Like we discussed earlier in the critique section, negative reviews should be treated in the same way. Don't react emotionally and respond, in writing, negatively to a negative review. Remember, the internet is forever, so if you respond to the reviewer and say they just didn't understand your book, or that they shouldn't have left a review at all, you're asking for trouble. Think of it as like throwing a match on gasoline. Instead, use those same coping techniques you use for negative critiques and review with fresh eyes.

If you want to respond (and can), go for it. Goodreads allows authors to like and/or comment on reviews, which is a great way to interact with readers and to show audiences you're listening. Sarah once received a three star, with a comment that said how the reader would have given her a one star, but he knew it was her first book and enjoyed the story even though there were many bumps along the way. Sarah responded that she really appreciated his honesty and hoped that he would still follow her journey as her writing career grew. Did he respond to her? No, but it's out there and it's those efforts other readers will see. When Sarah saw the review, did she question her writing abilities? You betcha. Did she reach for *The Animal Court* to start ripping it apart for the thousandth time, hell-yeah. But, she took a walk and reminded herself that reviews are subjective and that his review wasn't all that off; it was her first book and there were many growth opportunities within, so she was indeed very grateful for his honesty.

Every writer gets negative reviews. Everything as maddening as, "this book sucks" to, "there's too many characters," to, "I was triggered by the mugging in chapter 3, why doesn't this book have a trigger warning?" to "I'm only giving this one star because despite the well-written dialogue, and complex plot, the guard mentioned in chapter 3 and then again in 9 changed his eye color from brown to green; showing the author's lack of attention to detail. Otherwise, I loved the book!" Also, just as maddening are the one and two star reviews without explanation.

There will be scathing reviews. Trolls are real. They may not live under bridges, but they exist on the internet. Additionally, people are more likely to talk about the negative than the positive. But what's important, as author Pamela Jane explained in a Writers Digest article,[1] is to not "obsess" over those negative comments. Don't let those trolls get into your head. Instead, Jane suggests you try to find something to laugh about the negative reviews. There are reviews on books such as, "I bought this thinking it was science fiction, but it's a rom-com, so I gave it a one star." There's nothing that can be done with it except laugh, make a positive slanted comment back like, "Oh no! So sorry!" or just ignore it.

But we would challenge you to read the reviews, especially the negative ones. There can be information in them that will make you into a better writer. Perhaps you have a plot problem or your secondary characters aren't as well constructed as they could be. Maybe your conclusion at the end of your nonfiction book doesn't match up with what you planned the book to be, or perhaps you were repetitive. All of this information can help you be a better writer and shouldn't be discounted.

Rejections

Rejections are unfortunately a part of this writing world, unless you completely self-publish. A rejection means that you've sent a query to someone asking them to be your agent, your editor or to publish your book/short story and they've said, "no thanks." It can be doubly difficult because querying requires you to do research into these industry experts and what they're looking for. Each query is generally asking for something different, such as a 750-word bio rather than a 500-word bio and not following the instructions** can immediately cause them to reject you. Typos and misspelling people's names are just as bad and require attention-to-detail that's difficult when you're trying to balance out your life. Unfortunately, you HAVE to query to move forward in this business, which means you're going to get rejections.

Theresa: *Following the instructions is super important. Don't assume that because your story is "different" they'll change the rules for you. They won't and will reject you.*

So how can you keep engaged when another "no thanks" makes you feel like none of this is worth it?

- Vary what you're querying. Rather than just querying that novel you've spent half your lifetime on, try querying for some short stories. Even if your payment is just a copy of the anthology, getting a "win" on these types of queries can be empowering.
- Vent to your friends, your author friends. This is where having your tribe comes into play. You need others going through the rejection process to compare to, cry to and celebrate wins with.
- Turn it into something fun. We've mentioned the Race for Rejection on the Semi-Sages of the Pages Discord channel, but it bears repeating. Every rejection is a "point" and the person with the most "points" at the end of the year "wins". This is clever because it forces people to continue to query while celebrating those losses. There's a unique feeling to the dread of a rejection, followed by the, "a point for me!"
- Understand it's part of the process. Stephen King was rejected many times before he got wins for short stories in paid markets such as Playboy.

Querying is one of the most dreadful elements of publishing, including queries for articles and short stories. Receiving note after note after note saying things like:

- "Your book was great, but it's just not a good fit for us at this time."
- "Thank you for your submission, unfortunately, we are flooded with submissions and are just not able to accept any more at this time."
- "This just isn't marketable."

These rejections are generic. They're likely copied and pasted from a form letter. At times, you do get golden rejections like this:

- "We loved your story, but YA sci-fi just isn't selling right now. Submit again in three years."
- "Your story needs some developmental edits, and the climax didn't match the promises set out in the beginning. Make some changes and resubmit."
- "While we truly loved this story, we couldn't find a place in our anthology this time around. Resubmit at the next call and we'll see if we can find a place."

These are helpful, but can be disappointing too. Too many rejections can begin the negative spiral of asking ourselves, are we cut out for this? Are we actually good writers? Are we pursuing the right dream?

First, you are. If writing is all you think about, you are a writer dagnabbit, and that is what you should do.

Second, querying is both a marathon and a numbers game, as Morrigan Puhr, one of the hosts of the Semi-Sages of the Pages has said many times.

Not Meeting your Expectations

Writing is a tough world, one most people don't realize. We wish we could convey this difficulty better, but words like "hard", and "tough" just aren't enough. Everyone knows this life is hard, but many authors, no matter how they define success, will tell you this is one of the hardest things they've ever done. Monetary success can be fleeting, if it happens. And for those of you saying the art world, the acting world and the music world are the same—you're correct. Being a creative and finding monetary success is very difficult and takes an element of luck.

So what do you do, when you're not meeting your sales goals, number of social media followers or can't get that book deal?

- Talk to other people at the same stage you're at. Make writer friends at conferences, in critique groups or on social media. The key to this, is to make friends at the same stage you're at. Someone with dozens of books and an option for a streaming show will have different frustrations than someone querying. That disparagement can increase the feelings of failure and frustration.
- Focus on the creative part rather than the marketing and the sales. The best way to increase your sales to get your next project out there. Keep writing, keep focusing on that and perhaps your sales will change.
- Get an easy win. It may not directly help your sales figures, but easy wins such as hitting a certain number of followers on social media may give you a mental win. However, don't rely too much on this as there's not a direct correlation

between the number of followers on Facebook and the number of sales. There is a dotted line between the two, however.

- Go easy on yourself and stop comparing yourself with others. There are a handful of stories out there about writers who got that million dollar book deal for their first book and then went on to have amazing writing careers. There are many, many other stories of writers who never got past the querying stage or despite having a dozen books out, can't make ends meet. And then there are stories of authors who got that million dollar book deal, and their book was a flop, ruining their career. If you're going to compare, look at everyone! And remember with "success" can come other challenges.

- Change your expectations. It's easy while toasting your friends at your first book launch to think the sky's the limit. But the reality is different; perhaps your goal to be 100% financially secure on your writing isn't possible this year. Maybe it'll be possible next year. Keep trying, but it's ok to change your expectations if you need to.

Setbacks

Setbacks in the writing and publishing industry are endemic. There's printing problems, shipping problems, program errors, scams, predators, people who take on too much and can't deliver by the deadline. We know of several authors whose editors or cover artists disappeared in the night. Those last-minute changes, those micro details on a cover matter, but if the cover artist ghosts you, then what?

We've seen partial deliverables, outright failures, and people who oversold their abilities. Specifically seeing so many people she knew encountering the cover setback was a big part of the reason Sarah became a cover artist.

So let's hone in on one example of what can happen.

You've decided to DIY your cover. You've done your research on the covers trending in your genre for weeks and you're a graphic designer, a master of art and craft. Your cover looks amazing. Like, award winning-level. Your friends and fans cannot wait to see it on their shelves. You go to upload it to Amazon and then...

Rejected.

Something is off in your formatting and you don't know what. You followed their instructions to the letter, but you're still getting those red flags or your cover is so big you can't see 2/3rds of it. So now you spend hours troubleshooting to fix it before you can launch the pre-order you've been promising for weeks, on your social media and in your newsletter.

True story.

Theresa: *Someday, we will laugh about the mistake that pushed publishing this book into our forefront, pushing back several other deadlines and causing a great deal of stress. While that day is not today, we will blog about it, because we believe in transparency with our mistakes. And it was a great learning opportunity.*

The moral of this story is, you're going to have setbacks, and this is the time where it's going to likely be THE most frustrating. Many moons ago, Sarah became so frustrated with trying and failing to upload to Amazon that she essentially quit writing for a year. A year. Don't be like Sarah in the early days of her career. There are now so many resources available to you to help you through the riddles of these annoying setbacks. Try Facebook groups about whatever program or distributor you're trying to use. Try finding the actual people behind Adobe–they're there! These setbacks will happen and they'll take you down different roads than you ever thought you'd see. What's important is learning from these experiences.

The authors of this book have encountered just about every setback you can imagine. From major fires delaying Sarah's shipments of *The Animal Court* from arriving on time for her book launch, to Theresa shipping the books she needed for an event the next day to Sarah's house (she lives 90 minutes away).

From these mistakes, Sarah learned to ship books well before she launches. If possible, she tries to have at least ten author copies two weeks before the launch so she has some stock on hand.

Theresa learned to double check addresses before ordering (ok, she really learned to double check the details, especially when tired, but that's a lesson she's still working on)

As you emerge from these setbacks, write down the tricks and tips, keep them handy or along with your goals. Honestly, a good portion of this book are lessons of what we've learned from our setbacks. If something isn't working, adapt. The point is these setbacks, unfortunately, are how many of us learn and grow. Don't think of these moments as deal breakers or as signs from the universe you're not supposed to be published. Think of them instead as the universe helping you to learn something new.

Life Happens

In the year before publishing this book, both of Sarah's cats passed away. Her cats were her children. The hole left in her heart is immeasurable and she still gets very emotional whenever she thinks about them. She literally felt like she was hit by a train when her Bella passed away and she couldn't do *anything* for quite some time. She felt tremendous guilt for missing deadlines on top of mourning for her child, but after some time passed she realized that it's ok.

If you lose someone or something precious to you, you need to mourn. You need to heal. Life happens and sometimes it REALLY freaking sucks.

These hits from left field are all a part of the journey, hokey as that sounds. Find ways to deal with them healthily, and the smaller bumps in the road like a computer program crash will seem like nothing.

the end of this book is your beginning

Congratulations! You've made it through the book and may be feeling overwhelmed with the advice and exercises. So here's some more advice; take five exercises (or if you didn't do the exercises) five things that you found intriguing after reading this book. Then find another five that you're interested in, but you're ok not implementing immediately.

Set a goal to implement those five things immediately. They can be as easy as setting up a reward system for yourself, or as complex as hiring a neighborhood teenager to watch your kids. Give yourself two weeks, really trying those things. Put a reminder on your calendar and let us know on our No Bad Books Press, LLC Facebook Page how it's going for you.

At the end of two weeks, reassess. Were you able to follow through on those five things? Were they helpful or did you end up doing them for a day, and then a crisis hit and you stopped? Are they things you'd like to try again or are you completely abandoning them?

If you integrated or abandoned those five things, would you like to try an additional five things? If not, it's ok. It's not like we're looking over your shoulder or grading you.

This life and the choices you make are up to you. You decide what to try and what doesn't work for you.

You likely noticed how we asked you to check back in with your goals throughout this book. Your goals are your bedrock. Never lose sight of them. You are an incredible individual for picking up a craft that is exceptionally tricky. Let your goals be your north star. If you keep them in mind, they will guide you through the roughest patches of the darkest nights.

Your tools and resource kit is your own and something you'll have to experiment with to figure out what fits best for you. As a part of your journey, listen to the recommendations of others, but don't feel like you're chained to them or feel like you're failing because someone else's ace in the game isn't working for you. We offer our suggestions because they just might be phenomenal for you or they may not, but we hope our tips will at the very least inspire you to try something new.

One more note about this book. When Theresa taught childbirth classes in another life, she would tell her students that attending an 8-hour Saturday class wasn't enough. If they wanted to handle labor until they could get their epidural or all the way through, they had to practice the breathing, positions, exercises and massage techniques. Or it wouldn't work. Think about it like this... for those of you who played sports or a musical instrument... how much time did you spend practicing for that few minutes or an hour? You spent hours, and hours. Being a successful author is the same thing. You have to practice, you have to try, and you have to fail in order to succeed.

One of the biggest items you need to be successful is an understanding of this ever-changing industry and the acknowledgement that it will change. So you have to keep growing and learning. That book you read a year ago that helped you to grow tremendously may not be relevant or perhaps your understanding has increased beyond it. So don't stop learning; listen to podcasts, read lots of books in and outside your genre, and read books on craft and publication. Follow other authors who are your definition of successful and understand what they're doing. Attend conferences, go to those networking events, think about crafts and make friends with other authors. You will grow and learn so much; you may not recognize the person you were when you started this journey.

So, if you're still wondering, how do you really measure success or know when you're a successful author? Well, part of that has to do with your goals, but the key to this life, to being a successful author in whatever way you define it, is not to give up. You are a successful author when you keep going, you keep writing because, as Theresa says, if you write, you are a writer. We cannot emphasize that enough. You are a success because you are pursuing knowledge on your craft. You are a success because you're still going. You are a success because you tried something new, whether it worked. Your tenacious spirit is pursuing your dream. And that's pretty special.

Whatever your goals are for your writing, we hope this book provides a few insights or helps you on your journey. Let us know how you're doing by dropping us a line at nobbpress@gmail.com or on our Facebook Page or in our Semi-Sages of the Pages Discord Channel. If you have any ideas or tricks you changed, tell us! Maybe we'll include them in a future edition of this book!

Thanks for reading and all the best to you on your journey!

-Theresa and Sarah

authors note

We know, wasn't this entire book an author's note? But something happened in 2022, that Theresa wanted to speak to.

My wonderful son, Connor, is engaged to an amazing woman, Makayla. And her family is incredible. In the summer of 2022, Makayla's grandmother, Sharon, died suddenly. What made Sharon unique and something to discuss in this book is that she had many dreams and plans for the future. And one of those included seeing her memoir from her time as a new bride when her husband was over-seas in Vietnam, published. She'd connected with me several times to discuss the writing world, and a few days before she died, sent me a package about a writing confer-ence she wanted us to attend together. I received it the day after she died. I'm including this story at the end of this book because the one commodity that's limited is time. So if your dream is to get that memoir out, please do so. Now. Put this book down and start. If your dream is to be on the New York Times Bestseller list, time to start your research on how to get there. If you want to finish that ten-book fantasy series, get going! The time will pass whether you spend it pursuing your dreams, or hanging out on TikTok. Make the most of what you have!

notes

Introduction

1. An imprint is essentially your publishing brand and company; it's that cute little symbol you see on the spine and back of books. It's the name of a press that ISBNs are registered to. Our imprint is No Bad Books Press, LLC and we have the insignia of a hand holding a quill in a neat, rectangular frame.

1. Where and How do you Get Started?

1. Defined by the romance writers of America, "books issued under a common imprint/series name that are usually numbered sequentially and released at regular intervals, usually monthly, with the same number of releases each time." They are shorter and don't have a long shelf life.

2. How do you actually get published?

1. For more information, see the article Over the Past 25 Years, the Big Publishers Got Bigger—and Fewer by Jim Milliot published by Publisher's Weekly, Apr 19, 2022.
2. "What is a Small Press? (And Should Authors Use Them?)" published by Reedsy on February 2, 2020.
3. Learn more about agents at Publishers Marketplace
4. From the IBPA Advocacy Committee's Hybrid Publisher Criteria published in February of 2018.

3. How do you Find Inspiration/Ideas?

1. From the Master Class by David Baldacci: https://www.masterclass.com/classes/david-baldacci-teaches-mystery-and-thriller-writing/chapters/finding-the-idea-c213b7f2-8367-4ae4-9bba-2f7e94528ecc
2. That's the game when you pick a table, watch the people for a little while and imagine a whole life based on their actions, body language and if you can hear what they're saying.

4. How Do You Stay Motivated?

1. Some writers swear warm water helps them focus and get past writer's block. Even washing the dishes can help if you're stuck.
2. "Feel Like A Fraud" by Kirsten Weir published by the American Psychological Association, November 11, 2013.
3. "Why Taking Vacation Time Could Save Your Life" by Caroline Castrillon published by Forbes in may 23, 2021.

5. How Do You Actually Sell Books?

1. Drugs, various medications and trauma can also do this.
2. "Social media break improves mental health, study suggests" article published by the University of Bath on May 6, 2022.

6. But there's only 24-hours in a day–how do you do all of this?

1. Even though we broke it up into hours in a day, this method works well if you don't think about it on a daily basis. So you might plan for 35 hours a week of writing, but do three ten-hour days, and one five-hour day. You may get your 14 hours of chores/errands done on a weekend or do a little bit each day.
2. Yes, traffic in Southern California and in other places can be that bad! It's not an urban legend that we, like others, measure distance in time. "Even though that restaurant is fifteen miles away, it's going to take me an hour to get there; I don't want to go," happens all the time.
3. "How Multitasking Affects Productivity and Mental Health" by Kendra Cherry published by Very Well Mind on July 30, 2021.

7. But how do you Become a Successful Author?

1. "5 Tough Tips for Surviving (and Triumphing Over) Really Rotten Book Reviews" by Pamela Jane published by Writers Digest on December 8, 2018.

acknowledgments

This book and all the knowledge we've gained would not have been possible without the incredible writing community that has helped to guide us on our journeys. We mentioned numerous organizations, clubs, courses, and authors throughout this book and we'd like to extend an enormous thank you to each and every one of them. In no particular order, these superheroes include but are not limited to:

Tamara Merrill

Jerry Strayve Jr.

M.S. Ewing

Morrigan Puhr

Chris Bannor

Anna Bushi

David Green

Dennis K. Crosby

Judy Reeves

Lara Yamada

K.A. Fox

Izabela Markus

Catherine Pomeroy

Emily Harstone

Stephen King

Mark Dawson

Bryan Cohen

Gail Carrier

Christopher Locke
Stephen Green
L.S. Johnson
Elizabeth Gilbert
Joanna Penn
Annie Dillard
Writers Crutch
Margaret Atwood
Master Class Lesson with David Baldacci
Jonathan Maberry and the Writers Coffeehouse
Publishers Marketplace
Reedsy
Independent Book Publishers Association
The San Diego Writers and Editors Guild
San Diego Writers,
Ink the Independent Book Publishers Association
The San Diego Chapter of the Horror Writers Association.

If we missed you, please let us know and we'll be happy to
make a revision.

also by theresa halvorsen & s. faxon

The Animal Court by S. Faxon

Dad's Playbook to Labor & Birth by Theresa Halvorsen

Foreign & Domestic Affairs by S. Faxon

Lost Aboard by S. Faxon and Theresa Halvorsen

Origins by S. Faxon

Released Edited by Theresa Halvorsen and S. Faxon

River City Widows By Theresa Halvorsen

Warehouse Dreams by Theresa Halvorsen